# The Disregarded Witness

# T he Murder of Olof Palme and the Estonia Catastrophe

## The Secrets Unveiled

# Robert Barestrand

# *The Disregarded Witness*

# **T**he Murder of Olof Palme and the Estonia Catastrophe

## *The Secrets Unveiled*

© 2025 Robert Barestrand (ansvarig utgivare)

Korrekturläsning: Christopher Sjölund, Mette Mork
Ytterligare medverkande: Els-Marie Tidelius, Tobias Henricsson

Förlag: BoD · Books on Demand, Östermalmstorg 1, 114 42 Stockholm, bod@bod.se
Tryck: Libri Plureos GmbH, Friedensallee 273, 22763 Hamburg, Tyskland

ISBN: 978-91-8080-897-2

# Contents

# Preface

This document is based on Robert's untold story and his recollections regarding events that culminated in the murder of Olof Palme. The material itself is partly taken from recorded interviews that were conducted in proximity of the scene of the murder.

We who have helped Robert to get his story in print are only interested in getting the truth out about the murder of Prime Minister Olof Palme. Robert himself has made several attempts to share his information with the police, the first time being as early as 1986, and a subsequent last attempt in April 2018, when he met with Sven-Åke Blombergsson (investigator). The police have never taken Robert's information seriously.

It is therefore somewhat hilarious that the investigation, abbreviated in Swedish as the PU, was discontinued in quite a bizarre manner. In short, Stig Engström, was presented as the perpetrator during a highly anticipated press conference on 10th of June 2020. It was obvious the investigation had been directly influenced by the author of "The unlikely murderer", Thomas Pettersson. Moreover, that which was actually put forward was certainly nothing else but old material. Engström had been at the focal point early on in the investigation and subsequently dismissed as a suspect. Private investigator Olle Minell put some focus on Engström in a series of articles around 1989-1990, in a sense presenting back then what the prosecutor, Krister Petersson, chose to serve up in 2020. Furthermore it was accompanied by two blatant falsehoods.

Firstly Petersson proclaimed that witness Lars Jeppsson was sure the perpetrator wore a peaked cap, when in fact this was the detail Jeppsson was uncertain about. The detail Jeppsson was sure about was that the fleeing individual wore some sort of jacket, definitely not a coat. Secondly it was put forward that Engström checked out from his place of work after he had a shorter conversation with the security personnel manning the reception in the building. As the personnel testify, Engström left the building immediately after the conversation. Since his check out time was registered, it thus means there is no doubt that he had already swiped his card in the terminal when the conversation with the reception staff was initiated.

But for sure, it was no coincidence that Stig E left work at about 11:20 p.m. on that particular Friday night, Stig was part of the conspiracy but he didn't want to see the perpetrator carry out the murder. Every investigator should hate fortuity, as some ancient prophet once proclaimed. Robert had met Stig several times during the preparations, so he can actually present Stig with an alibi since Robert was the first to arrive at Olof Palme's body. Further on down the line Robert was destined to be labeled as "the stripling".

**<u>Prior to publication, this document has been approved by Robert Barestrand.</u>**

# Robert Barestrand's background and upbringing

Robert Barestrand was born on the 12th of November 1969 in Poland as Jacek Robert Baranowski, later changed to Jacek Robert Barestrand. Robert's family moved to Stockholm, Sweden, in the 1970's from Poland, while Robert himself came to Sweden around 1980/81. In Stockholm he lived independently of his parents during his early teens. After one year at Enskede Gårds gymnasium, Robert dropped out of school. He then learned to live life by himself, independent of parents and institutions following "the hard school of life" theorem.

Around 1985, when Robert was still in high school, one day as he was performing metalwork, the school's student assistant, **Håkan E**, shows up alongside Robert. He praises Robert and says that he has noticed that Robert seems handy at metal work. From here on he observes Robert's strengths and in time they become more and more acquainted with one another.

After some time, Robert is introduced to a friend of Håkan's named **Gunnar Ställfors**[1]. Gunnar lived in the Stockholm suburb of Alby at the time. Gunnar had a summer cottage in Norrtälje and also a boat (gig) that he "needed a ghost on".

Robert, who was a spirited, alert and adventurous person, liked to learn new things, and had also previously been a member of Mälarhöjden's scout troop. He had participated in the "Sailing Scouts" scheme, so he had some experience of seafaring. After a while, Robert began to travel with Gunnar on his boat, and Robert's way of handling the boat was much appreciated.

Håkan also had a boat, a sailing vessel, probably a Maxi-77 or some equivalent model. On one occasion Robert accompanied Håkan out to sea, and they came to moor north off Vaxholm. Around that time, Robert noticed that Håkan began to make some physical advances towards him. Robert rejected him, but still found it uncomfortable. Later they came to the island of Ilsholmen where Gunnar rented a cottage, which is on the way to Vätö. Robert went there on the weekends sometimes, to escape from life in the city and his alcoholic mother who didn't treat him fairly and kindly.

Robert had learned decent Swedish, being intelligent and clever, although he needed more help in school, especially with learning the Swedish language. Unfortunately, he didn't receive the help required. Gunnar noticed this, and the problems at home eventually led to Robert more or less moving in with Gunnar. One could say that he helped Robert develop as a person in Sweden.

Gunnar also had a lot of fun and exciting stuff, interesting books to read, as well as lots of videos to watch. In addition, Gunnar did a lot of fun things, which made life more comfortable and cheerful for Robert. Gradually, he learned more and more Swedish, and therefore managed his high school years better. Around the time of the murder, Robert was mostly in high school and with Gunnar, and from time to time even went home to visit his mother.

It turned out that Gunnar too had an attraction to young boys. Unfortunately, it was to some extent to the detriment of Robert, although no physical advances ever took place. He firmly rejected him, and this was respected. But from the beginning, the association was based on Robert feeling that he had nowhere to go, and therefore he had a safer life with Gunnar, who in some sense filled the roll as an "extra dad" and also to some extent as a mentor. Gunnar, in turn, may have felt that he had a "son" who could assist him in various small assignments and errands.

As for the planning of the murder, Robert didn't really understand what was going on. But he kept up with everything as best as he could, regarding what was going to take place. In general, he followed Gunnar and the gang in everything they were doing, and also came to assist a lot with practical things, even if he did not understand the purpose of what he was doing or the meaning of it. He learned much, and the time with Gunnar & Co was the entrance into the adult world for Robert.

# Prelude to the murder

Robert picked up a lot of what Gunnar and his accomplices were talking about, even if they didn't seem to comprehend this. With all these antics, he became more and more interested in listening to what they were talking about, and also remembered a lot of it. It should be noted that Gunnar had an office at Sparbanksvägen 4 in Hägersten. This was a former bank/post office with an associated vault, where he ran a company with various projects. Among other things, he bought another company that was involved in perfume, then he tried to produce an "animal shampoo", and also created a medicine against ringworm. Further on, he started a project to reprogram computers. None of these projects were particularly successful.

But Gunnar was best known for his work as a master of ceremonies at various events, as an entertainer at shopping malls, company parties, on the ferries and in radio programs, often appearing in various music contexts. The office became a base for his projects. Robert's hobby, on the other hand, was building model airplanes at that time, which he occupied himself with when he was in Gunnar's office.

At this office several different people often came to greet Gunnar. On the one hand, these were good friends, but there were also business partners and people with whom he collaborated on his various projects. Below are the people who had more or less connection to the Palme murder, but are not presented in any particular order of precedence. One of the friends he worked with was **Håkan E**, who can also be seen as a key figure in the planning.

*To be noted. Due to privacy and integrity issues, all the following names concerning the group, except for Gunnar Ställfors, are fictitious. Persons not directly associated with the group are presented with their actual names.*

Two of the acquaintances were **Thomas H** and **Jonas N**. They were "sailing adventurers" and also friends of Gunnar. In addition, Gunnar was visited by a programmer named **Joel Ö**, who worked with ABC80 computers. This Joel then recruited a guy named **Lars M**. Lars, in turn, knew a guy who Robert believes was called **"Jonas"**, Robert estimates that he was in his 20's at the time.

This "Jonas" was, according to Robert's recollection, to have worked as a computer expert for the police, and also assisted with programming computers on the behalf of Lars. "Jonas" also had some contacts in the police diving association, where Robert came to practice deep breathing along with "Jonas", at the premises in question. "Jonas" had been briefed in the police locker room that the Palme couple would be without bodyguards at the time of the planned assassination, and also when and how these would be moving around the city. Apparently, they found out at quite a late stage prior to the murder that Palme was going to the cinema that night. According to Robert, it happened just a few days before the murder.

Gunnar and Robert used to visit another friend of Gunnar's named **Rolf K**. This Rolf also became involved in the actual murder of Palme. Robert remembers one passage in particular that occurred at the planning stage of the murder. Rolf talked to Gunnar about someone named "Yvonne". Gunnar lived in a house next to Rolf's apartment building in Alby. Yvonne also lived in the same area. Yvonne and Rolf lived close to each other, they were almost neighbours, according to Robert. On that particular occasion, Rolf was discussing with Gunnar regarding this **"Yvonne"**. Rolf wondered, "can we trust her to show up at the right time and in the right place?". Rolf also knew that Yvonne (Nieminen) was dating a new boyfriend, presumably Ahmed Zahir.

Approximately two weeks before the murder, Robert and some of the group members were visiting a bank manager, **Bertil Albons**[2] , at what was then the SEB and the address being Sveavägen/Tegnergatan. Robert jokingly says about Olof Palme: "That bastard should be shot!", whereupon Gunnar looks suspiciously at Robert, perhaps worried that Robert might be suspecting something.

A few days before the murder, Robert remembers that there was feverish talk and planning regarding, what he later understood, the murder of Olof Palme. According to Robert, both Gunnar and Håkan E had a pronounced contempt for Olof Palme, even if it was not their contempt that was the motive behind the deed. Instead, it seems to have been a purely financially motivated act on their part.

At some point, Håkan from Gunnar's office called Palme, but he did not answer. Some time before the murder, Gunnar, Håkan E and Robert were riding in Gunnar's green Volvo 242 to the Old Town of Stockholm and parked outside the Royal Palace, at the large parking lot that was located there at the time.

Gunnar and Robert then entered into the Old Town, specifically to an old house that was at the back of a larger alley. There they stood, looking up at some windows of that house for perhaps 15 minutes. Thereafter, the two returned to the Volvo. Now Robert had to wait in the car while Gunnar and Håkan E went into the Old Town again. Robert assumes that they went back to the house he had just been outside off. However, he was not told why they were looking up at the house.

Some time before the murder, Robert remembers that some kind of forensic scientist came out to Gunnar's cottage on Ilsholmen and demonstrated how the police worked technically. It was a half-day "lecture" on how to secure trails, among other things.

## At the office in Hägersten, suburb to Stockholm

Prior to the murder, Håkan E had picked up cartridges in Hägersten from an arms dealer, but they were probably not the ones that came to be used. The ones used were thick and copper-collared and had something "blue" on them. Gunnar kept the weapon and bullets in a briefcase in the vault of his office. Robert remembers that they had test-fired the weapon before. Gunnar probably test-fired the weapon in Solna (suburb to Stockholm).

Robert once asked Gunnar if he was right-handed or left-handed, but according to what Robert remembers, Gunnar claimed that he was both, although he usually used his left hand. Robert remembers that when they were at the pillar before the murder, Gunnar held the revolver in his left hand as he loaded it. Another memory is that Håkan E one day before brought an ID card to Gunnar, but he didn't think it was good enough. It was probably an ID card that could be used at a shooting range.

Three people who could be labeled "Skandia men" came to Gunnar's home, where Robert also was at the time. The three men dressed in dark clothes got out of a black car that pulls up by the street. It was some type of vintage car from perhaps the 1940s/50s. It was very similar to a Citroën Traction Avant, or maybe an old Opel, according to Robert. Robert rides the elevator down with one of them after the meeting. He remembers that **Stig Engström**[3] took the stairs with another person which it was important that Robert did not get to see. At the time, Robert was also told to leave the apartment. He had to go up the stairs and "hide" higher up.

Robert's recollection of the three men: The first, an elegant gentleman who smelled of perfume whom he shared the elevator with. Later, Gunnar got a cap from the man, in which it was possible to conceal the yellow earmuffs. Håkan E and Jonas N were also present during that occasion. This was somewhere around the corner of the Skandia building in a kind of shop that we have given the working name "The Bakery Shop".

The second "Skandia man" may have been the tall man who recurs in Robert's story several times and could, according to him, be the man he meets when he makes his way past the barracks towards the Palme couple. The third person thus was **Stig Engström.**

# The week preceding the murder

During the planning stage, Gunnar, Robert and another, unknown man, were eating in a fancy restaurant on Djurgården in Stockholm. It was located beyond Gröna Lund and further out on Djurgården. The day after the restaurant visit, Gunnar and Robert visited Rolf. Rolf's participation was to ensure, among other things, guiding off the "tall lady" to the place together with a man. Rolf was to guard the south side, thereafter he came with the couple from the south side to the pillar, and ultimately went straight to the barracks. They were then in the barracks, on the ground floor. Gunnar exclaimed regarding Palme: "If I don't kill the fandom, the young people will kill him."

On one occasion, Robert doesn't really know how long before the murder, he went into the Skandia building. He then had to go up to Stig Engström's office, where he had to wait outside. He remembers that there was a blue carpet, a round table placed in an inner corner, as well as few chairs in the hallway.

At some point, Robert heard Stig Engström say to Gunnar, regarding the guards at the reception inside the Skandia building, that he was keeping an eye on them and that it would be all right. On another occasion Gunnar and Stig were in Stig's office while Robert had to wait downstairs in the foyer. After that visit, they drove off in Gunnar's car and Gunnar pointed out something about "the time" and looked at the clock at the House of Culture. Then he says this to Robert: "This is where time is controlled" and "This is how you gain 2 1/2 minutes. I wanted 5 minutes, but I couldn't." Robert doesn't know what he meant by this. It took place about a day before the murder.

In the morning on the same day of the murder, Gunnar and Robert drive to Uppsala. Well there, Gunnar met up with a member of the military. Robert remembers that this person might have held some important position. He lived in an apartment building. The meeting lasted for about 20 minutes and Robert was not allowed to go up to the military man, thus remaining in the car the whole time.

Later the same day, Gunnar "reports" himself in at some kind of military facility along the road at Söder Mälarstrand. "You had to sign up there before you started anything.", Gunnar exclaimed.

# Friday evening, February 28 – before the murder

Gunnar and Robert arrived at the bank manager Bertil Albon's office at around 6 p.m., and were thereafter supposed to drop Bertil off in Solna (suburb to Stockholm) at exactly 10:00 p.m. They drive into town on the road from Norrtull. They first stop at a parking lot on Sveavägen, between the cinema Grand and Adolf Fredrik's cemetery. Gunnar gets out and talks to Thomas H, who is standing by the pay phone. Gunnar says: "Now we're going to go and pick up Håkan at Vasagatan".

They proceed in driving towards Sergels Torg to pick up Håkan. They drive towards the glass pillar and turn right on the street behind the shopping mall Åhléns. They turn around behind it and come out on the south side of Vasagatan. There, Gunnar says: "Bring out what's there, under the seat". Robert holds it up between the seats and asks where to put it. Gunnar goes on to say something in the terms of "You know, this one has been around since 1955 something, and kept all in order. It will be useful to you one day. Place it on the seat." So Robert puts the revolver on the passenger seat. He noticed that the revolver was a little worn, not perfectly black. Robert wondered what Gunnar meant, and asked when he would "benefit" from it? Gunnar replies that when Robert gets older, maybe he will get calls about similar "jobs".

**Explanatory notes regarding subchapters 1-11**

The descriptions and experiences depicted are purely based on Robert's recollection of the events as they unfolded all those years ago, and how they ultimately culminated in the assassination of Olof Palme. Therefore, at times, the timeline may seem incoherent and the geography somewhat confusing.

Therefore, upon agreement with Robert, the unfolding of events will be presented in an unadulterated manner. Clarity and coherency are certainly objectives to strive for, though in this case the value of raw memories surpass those objectives.

After all, it is a testimony so close to the events it thereby must be justified to present the raw data as is.

### 1. Gunnar and Robert pick up Håkan E

Shortly afterwards, Håkan jumps into the car, where the revolver is. Håkan throws stuff into the back seat next to Robert – a white-grey patterned cloth bag, a plastic bag and a nice Canon camera.

Gunnar and Robert get out of the car. Robert stands there and waits for a while, as Gunnar walks away. After some time he sees that they have parked the green Volvo further away. Now Gunnar is returning. The bags are left in the car, as Robert, Gunnar and Håkan walk away along the sidewalk. They give the impression that they are three guys who have been out partying. After a while they split up, and Gunnar disappears. Robert and Håkan continue and approach the scene of the upcoming murder from the south.

They head north and before "The House of Culture" Gunnar sets off to the right. As Robert and Håkan continue, they cross over to the other side, at the church. Robert sits by the wall and waits while Håkan enters an apartment. Håkan comes back with Gunnar and thereafter Håkan disappears.

### 2. Robert asks Gunnar about what is going on

They go for a walk and Robert asks Gunnar what they are doing there. He learns that they are going to help Håkan train for a film shoot. "What are we going to do then?", Robert asks. They walk towards the stairs in Tunnelgatan, Gunnar points up the stairs and says to Robert, "You can count those steps. Maintain a moderate speed, or half-run."

Robert comes up the stairs. Once there he meets a couple strolling along. Then he starts to head back down, and on one of the ledges he meets a man who glares at him in a somewhat sourly manner. As Robert comes back down, Gunnar asks him to repeat the same with the escalator, to go up and then return down again. He was also instructed to turn left when he reached the top of the stairs, and then quickly proceed on to Malmskillnadsgatan north to meet up with Gunnar, specifically where the roads crossed. Only then did Robert realise that Gunnar was clocking the time when Robert was pursuing the different distances.

Robert soon also noticed that they had access to the yellow barracks. Apparently, they had also made sure that no guards came there for several hours. The guard wouldn't return again until after midnight.

**Bernt L** suddenly stood at the barracks with Håkan, and asked Robert the following: "Can you go and buy cigarettes over there - red Prince", pointing around the corner of a restaurant that was nearby. It was a restaurant with a white and blue sign, Robert recalls. The door was on the far right. When you came in, there was a bar straight ahead and it continued left. There were tables on the left side facing the window. The bar also continued right and there were tables there as well.

Bernt at some point enters into the upper floor of the barracks where he is said to have photographed and filmed the murder.

Håkan enquires about the surveillance camera. "Let's just take it down!", he proclaims. Håkan used the ladder that was under the scaffolding and turned down the camera.
"Are the guys deployed?" (Rolf, Jonas...) "The light is controlled from within."

There was a cable to an office/apartment in the building next door where you could turn off the street lights. Håkan had previously worked at Dekorima and had arranged for them to have necessary accesses.

They could enter the barracks from the south side, and Robert remembers what it looked like when one enters. Straight ahead there were some shelves, where Håkan's boat radio was placed, and to the left someone had glued the windows shut. He remembers that Gunnar was concerned about fingerprints. Up to the right by a valve was a cable that Gunnar said he could disconnect later. There was also a recreational room inside. The chairs were orange, and it was nice and warm there. This was on the ground floor. Robert himself never went to the upper barracks.

– Gunnar and I walked here on Tunnelgatan. I know he was standing here for a while, doing something with the person who was inside Dekorima (an art and crafts shop).
– Was there anyone inside?
– There was someone inside, Gunnar tapped on the Dekorima window and signaled to the man.
"The switchboard is located inside there", he said.
"And then we can turn on and off the lights as we please."

### 3. A phone call is placed on Luntmakargatan

"There was a payphone here somewhere on Luntmakargatan, a payphone that was mounted on the wall. The man who drove the "Hippie Bus" was there at the phone booth and called. Gunnar gave him money to call for. Robert also believes that he was at the consulate and probably came from Venezuela." Robert recalls the following:

*"There was a short elderly foreigner with a brown leather jacket standing by a wall mounted telephone. It had a cup over it. It belonged to Televerket (Swedish telephone company). "*

Robert then asked Håkan, "Who was that guy there?"
Robert thinks Gunnar gave the man money around then, and he was proceeding to call. But he was from Venezuela and mentioned Palme, who according to him had made it impossible to succeed in gaining freedom in his country, because the government had been supplied with weapons on the part of Palme.

23

– That s right, so he didn't like Palme?
– It didn't seem so, no.

"What shall I do?" Robert asked Gunnar. "You can go over to the middle of the blue house and come back."
Robert demonstrates how Gunnar pointed southwest across Sveavägen from the corner of the subway entrance opposite that of the former Dekorima shop. So Robert walked over, and came back. Then Robert stood here at the pillar. Then Robert sees a dark guy with a walkie-talkie appear behind the gate to the subway entrance. Håkan, who has the keys, opens the gate.

*To be noted. The dark guy appearing with a walkie-talkie in fact fits the description of the "Dekorima man" as the "Finnish girls" describe the person. Moreover, witness John Wiklund leaves as similar description of such an individual. It therefor can be assumed Wiklund and the women have observed the same person. Whereas Wiklund's observation is coherent to Roberts's location wise, the women seem to have mirrored their observation.*

– At the same time, almost, I think, a taxi is parked over here on the other side of the road. Pointing over Sveavägen. And the taxi driver comes across.

"Where am I going to drive this?", he asks.
"Drive it to the boathouse, to the club."
And then Håkan was handed a bag of food. The guy at the gate received something as well.

At one point, Lars and Joel came rushing up from the subway, and they had a brief meeting where they sat down in some dark place close to the barracks, apparently to sign some documents. And thereafter they were in the barracks and sat down for a while, enabling Robert to warm up a bit.

## 4. Gunnar loads the weapon

Gunnar, Håkan and Robert stood by the pillar. Sometime before the Finnish girls (the women who observed a Finnish speaking person with a walkie-talkie prior to the murder) arrived, Gunnar loaded the weapon there.

– Then I know, in one situation, Gunnar says to Håkan. "Stand here." And Gunnar is standing here, and I'm standing here. Robert articulates how they stand three people in a sort of circle close to each other, at the pillar, with their backs pointing outwards so that no one will see what they are doing? Shows how Gunnar picks up the weapon. "Look, here's how it's done."
– With the revolver?
– Yes! No one saw it, so to speak. Håkan is standing here with a blue jacket. And here's how to do it. I'll put them in here, but we won't put them all in, because then you can see. There was some reason, I don't remember this now. You wouldn't put all the cartridges in because then you could see .. if it was .. order. And you could do it in two different ways, either just "Boom-boom-boom" (in quick succession) or you charge and then you pull the trigger. It went equally well both ways and rapidly fires them off. – What kind of weapon was it then?

Earlier, in the car, Robert saw a revolver that Gunnar had, which was dated around the year 1955. The spout gleamed – the piston was brown and worn. But it is uncertain whether it was the one used for the murder. At the time of loading, Robert thought that the weapon looked more blackish.

– It was a bigger 357, I can tell you that.
– It was like that?
– Yes, yes.
– Do you remember what the ammo looked like, roughly?
– It was like this. Shows the length and width, about 3 cm, and 1 cm, between the thumb and index finger. Thick bullets he picked up loose from his coat pocket.
– And how many do you think he loaded?

– He didn't load all of them in. I think he saved two or something. Because she (Mrs. Palme) just received a warning shot. He didn't mean to shoot her. She got herself a warning shot. That was enough.
– The cartridges he took from the bank vault. They were the ones he used. Håkan was in his office.
– After we were working on the weapon, Gunnar walked over here. Robert points towards the corner of the Dekorima shop. Then Håkan says to me "You can run over and stand over there", pointing across Sveavägen to the west.

### 5. Håkan and Robert are waiting for the phone to sound

"Run over somewhere". – And I'm taking a short cut like this. I don't know where the pedestrian crossing was then, because I know I didn't give a damn about the pedestrian crossing. I just ran across, diagonally across here. And so I stood and waited there.

Describes that he is standing on the other side of the road a little further away on the north sidewalk of Tunnelgatan.

– Shortly after, Håkan arrives. At the same time as we're over there, Lars comes running. It seemed to me that he was coming from across the street. Then looking to the pavement on the west side of the Skandia building there was another guy standing there. And then yet another person standing there, with the nice shoes.

And then he explains. "It's happening" in other words, everything. " Ok, but then I'll go around the other way later."

*Håkan and Robert go up to an apartment located on the west side of Sveavägen opposite the Skandia building.*

– I'm waiting in the hallway, but I went to the window too. Håkan is sitting in the kitchen, it's on the right side. And then there is an opening between the kitchen and the living room. And he's crouched down there, waiting for the phone to ring, looking out, and then I'm looking out too. From there you had a good view of Sveavägen and the Skandia building.


## 6. Thomas calls and confirms, the couple is approaching

– "Yes, no, let's go!" says Håkan. He and Robert run down and through the subway and reemerge at the corner opposite of Dekorima.
– And I know there were some cars there, pointing across Sveavägen. There were a few cars that were going here. And then I parried, I walked in front of or behind them.
– Do you remember what colour the cars were?
– No. But there were a few craftsman cars.
– There were a few cars running red lights. I walked behind them, and Håkan too. Then we came back here. I was so surprised that you could walk under the street and come up at the subway exit near Dekorima. I didn't think much about it, coming up here. Gunnar is standing there, pointing towards Tunnelgatan. Gunnar comes up to us here, and says that "There were some Finnish women here, but I scared them off." "But what's going to happen?" asks Håkan, "Can't they call or something?"
"Fuck them, there's nothing over there," Gunnar replies.
– Now the Palme couple are on their way. So we set ourselves up. Håkan and I, we must have been standing somewhere here, kind of. Stands to the left off the pillar, as seen from Dekorima, facing the scene of the murder.

## 7. Rolf arrives with a couple, they return to the barracks


Rolf arrived at the future murder scene from the south in a car, accompanied by a tall woman and a shorter man. The car stopped at the pillar opposite to the scene of the murder, and the three went straight to the barracks. They were mainly housed in the barracks on the ground floor. They had access to the yellow barracks, and they had also made sure that no guard came there for several hours. Robert later learned that this woman's name was **Ann-Kristin Wallenberg**[4].

A younger man[5] with a backpack, headphones and suede blue jacket, first passed the couple, pushed past closest to the wall and continued north on the east side of Sveavägen.

Håkan covered me, here. I shouldn't check, he thought.

– But did you see Palme then?
– Yes!
– How far away would you say they were when you stood here?
– I would say that they were before that brown sticking out there, something like that.
– And where does Gunnar stand
– Somewhere in here. Points at Dekorima window side, on Tunnelgatan. He had contact with a person inside there, somehow.
– Could it have been that he knocked that "now they are over there"? So maybe it was two guys?
– I had no idea, but he was afraid that he had left marks there on the window, somehow.

## 8. Håkan and Robert walk up to Luntmakargatan and turn left

– But Håkan and I are standing here. I walk back to the pillar and he covers me. And at one point, he says, "Come on!" And I start walking then, but he says, "Let's play a little bit like this." So he went on like this and zigzagged across the street.
– Can you show us what it looked like?
– We were about to laze around like this.

Robert shows how Håkan skipped across Tunnelgatan to the east, in zigzags.

– And then we continued here.
– How fast did you go?
– Maybe a bit like this, "come along!" jumped/half-ran. I was a bit slow there. So we continue here, with Håkan.
– Here at Luntmakargatan we walk at a normal pace.

## 9. Shots are fired and the assassination is a fact

– Ok, we are walking here, walking north along the western sidewalk on Luntmakargatan. Somewhere, we hear the revolver shots BOOM! BOOM! And Håkan jumps up, happy: "Damn, now it's New Year's Eve "So it was a hell of a firework display! Then we proceeded. We'll get further away here, maybe here. "No, but we're going too far now," says Håkan. So we start going back south. Somewhere around here we meet Gunnar who is walking at a brisk pace. We stand together for a short time while Gunnar picks up cartridges and what he has left in his pocket. And Håkan puts it in a plastic bag, as far as I can remember.
– What colour was it then?
– Also white and red. And I think he got a plastic bag from Håkan, and Gunnar showed him this: "I've already got my pants underneath," bends forward and pulls one of his trouser legs up somewhat. There were white pants underneath. And I think he had the jacket underneath as well. That's why he appeared so fat and plump. And then he was wearing other dark shoes. Gunnar then changed into his light clothes, inside the gate at the back of the Skandia building.
– I know I'm going back with Håkan here.
– Gunnar, he continued, pointing north on Luntmakargatan. We return here, with Håkan, quite quickly. And I know I was looking back up up north. And then Gunnar disappears through the door, into the Skandia building. I was so surprised. How the hell can he know about a door there? That was something new to me. Ok, going further south. We'll arrive somewhere here. Then suddenly, I'm standing here. I think I remember standing in the middle of the barracks, at the long side of the barracks, on the north side. I was standing here like a fucking idiot.
– Håkan says: "wait here". He rounds the barracks, points counter clockwise around the barracks, running over there somewhere, to the stairs, pointing to the stairs to the east. And then I see here, that there is Rolf, the tall guy. He had probably passed the murder scene and then walked south of the barracks. Then Håkan comes back to me. " Oh well, come here, come here!" Håkan tried to make Robert move faster. "Come here now," he tells me because I'm a fucking fool. So I'll be standing here somewhere. Then he says to me: "Look what's happened there, why don't you run over and have a look!" Pointing towards the

murder scene. At the same time, I look back, pointing towards the stairs. Then I see both of them, running up the stairs. And, there was some fucking wimp too, over there somewhere.

– Wimp?

– Yes, there was some guy standing there, just staring like this. He also wore a blue jacket.

– Was he standing behind or before the barracks or..?

– I just know that somewhere I saw in my memory that there was someone standing and watching the whole thing. I know that Håkan glared at him when he passed by him.

– Ok, so you can see that there's someone standing there. It should have been **Lars Jeppsson**.

– Yes, but Håkan continues, and almost at the same time, I would say, they go up the stairs, both[6] Rolf and Håkan.

– Both of them?

– Yes! Straight up! Pointing with his whole arm towards the stairs. When Håkan passes me here, then, before I head off towards the murder scene, I meet a gentleman, who looks at me.

The man Robert met at the time of the murder, half-running after Gunnar, was neither Christer Pettersson, Stig Engström nor the man Robert had previously met with Gunnar behind the Skandia building. As Robert ran toward the murder scene, he looked at Robert, and Robert remembers his face. "The one who half-ran after Gunnar was tall, wore a black cap, black clothes (a flapping thin overcoat and trousers), black shoes, and generally was neatly dressed. He didn't wear glasses. It wasn't one of the Skandia guys, definitely not Stig".

Robert never saw the person in question again.

– And I meet the man here somewhere. He comes from that direction, points to Dekorima and looks at me like this, almost offended. And then I continue out there towards the murder scene.

– Where did he retreat, this man. Robert ponders and points back to the man he'd just met. I don't know, honestly.

– But according to Jeppsson, the supposed assassin fled upwards. Someone ran up the stairs.

– Yes, Rolf and Håkan. Håkan continued his damn jog up there on the

ridge pointing up the stairs to the east, while Rolf later picked me up, pointing towards the scene of the murder. Rolf came down the hill where I had clocked Gunnar. Comes here, shows with his arm how he came down counter clockwise around Skandia back to the scene. That's what the old lady, Lisbeth, told me "someone had come by who didn't bother to help". I set off here, pretty quickly, but only in the beginning it was icier here. But then it was ice free here.
– And what happens when you come running?
– I'm coming here, to the murder scene.

## 10. Robert arrives at Olof Palme after the shooting

When he first arrives, he sees no cars and no people except for the Palme couple. Lisbeth is upset, so he tries to calm her down. He remembers that he learned that you should not do CPR if help can come within 5-8 minutes. He sits down next to Olof and feels that there is still a pulse to be found. Then **Stig Engström** shows up and helps him to put Olof in a forward prone side position towards the corner, away from Dekorima, so that his head is lower, because he had learned that at the camp on Blidö. Stig then leaves Robert and runs into Tunnelgatan eastwards. Stig[7] probably wanted to talk to the perpetrator, whom he knew so well.

While he's sitting there, 2 girls arrive from the south. At the same time, he sees that there are some men standing behind him, at the corner. One of the girls, **Anna Hage**, turns Olof around and asks Robert "do you know this?", referring to CPR.

"Very well" he replies and starts looking for the bottom ribs of Olof. He then does compressions. But at some point, he also says, "You shouldn't do this", because that's what he'd learned. He notices that there are a few people standing behind him.

**Note to be considered:** *Hage actually mentions this episode in her interrogation on the 2th of April 1986. According to her, someone proclaimed, "why are you doing like this, I know he should be in a position of prone side". Furthermore, Hage also mentions that a* *person started "jerking with the victims legs". Hage then rebuffed the individual in question. Robert certainly interacted with Hage verbally, though he was not the person attempting to reposition the injured Olof Palme. It is therefore asserted that Robert was first at the scene with Hage, though the identity of the individual that physically tried to intervene remains unknown. No witness has claimed to be the person "jerking with Palme's legs".*

Another person says, "He can't do this, get rid of him!", "Get out of here!".

Instead, Anna Hage continues with compressions and Robert has to do mouth-to-mouth resuscitation and blow in air. He gets all bloody and sticky around the mouth.

At one point, he notices that a couple is standing on Tunnelgatan in the direction of the barracks, watching. The woman is taller than the man, the woman and the man who had arrived earlier on. Possibly the man was a driver. Then Robert sees them out of the corner of his eyes.

***Note to be considered:*** *Hage also observed a couple as she was leaving the vehicle she was travelling in. The couple in question at that instance were positioned north of the scene of the murder. They have never been identified to this day. It could therefore be assumed it was the same couple as Robert observed.*

### 11. Robert leaves the scene of the murder

As Robert was subsequently chased away, he instead went and stood by the pillar. Rolf came from the north along Sveavägen having rounded the block. He was tall and thin, wearing a "long, flimsy coat, yellowish beige in the style of cowboys." He must have been the "tall beige" man that Lisbeth has described that did not want to help her. Then Rolf came up to Robert and picked him up: "Come here now," he said, and they continued walking south along the east side of Sveavägen.

Soon they meet Gunnar coming out from the left somewhere, Robert doesn't recall where. Gunnar is wearing white clothes and gives the impression that he has been drinking beer. At some point, Gunnar looks at the clock and says, "We've got a good 7 or 9 minutes now." Soon after, Gunnar enters a gate on the left side, in the building along the crossroads. Inside the gate, mailboxes hang along the right-hand wall. Gunnar goes up the stairs, and then he comes back and says, "He wasn't home." Robert doesn't know what they're doing there, but he sees Gunnar throwing something in one of the mailboxes.

Gunnar, Rolf and Robert continue walking and Robert overhears one of them repeating the name "Magnusson" several times. They move on and Gunnar and Rolf discuss which side of Sveavägen they should walk on when they cross the street. Robert perceives that it has to do with how well they could be seen when the police would come driving towards the crime scene. They walk further ahead and Gunnar says that the police took the other way.

They cross the road on the left and continue onto the road to the left, towards the bridge. There is almost no traffic there then. On the way there, Rolf or Gunnar says that "Håkan should already have been here, why isn't he here?" They continue towards the bridge. Gunnar's Volvo is parked on the right side of the road, and there are several other cars there as well.

Then the couple Robert had seen earlier, the tall woman and the shorter man, come walking on the other side of the road. They seemed to have been having a beer or a glass of champagne. They had a parked pickup truck by the road.

Robert and the others wait for the couple to get away. When Håkan finally gets there, he complains that he has had to run so much "up there". Gunnar and Rolf leave with the car. Håkan and Robert walk back towards Sveavägen.

Gunnar had said that if the police came, they would see Robert and Håkan because the car was lighting up the road, so they went over to the north side and continued out towards Sveavägen. Then they cross the road and continue along the north side of Kungsgatan. Håkan and Robert cross the road again and enter Hötorget. In the far right corner of the square, the south corner, there is a hippie bus visible, and all alone. At some point, Robert is allowed to get into the bus and wipe the blood from his mouth.

At the same time, a car turns in from Olofsgatan opposite the square, they had taken a turn and rounded the cemetery. In the car is Lars and a man with low-heeled shoes who apparently has to pay, Robert will find out later on.

They walk down to the corner where the bus is and continue walking west on Gamla Brogatan. At some point, Robert says to the others, "You weren't going to kill him!"

*Note to be taken. There exists witness reports confirming that someone exclaimed that particular sentence.*

From Gamla Brogatan they turn right onto Drottninggatan. There is a car parked at the far end of Klarabergsgatan along the left side, but facing north towards Kungsgatan. It's a red Italian sports car with chrome trim on the back. The car had dark yellow leather seats. The guy who has the car takes his time and opens the bonnet to show something, he also opens the trunk and there are some chrome strips that "need to be fixed". The guy's name was probably Jörgen. He was the one who paid some of the money. Robert believes that they brought a briefcase, which Lars took care of.

Afterwards, they walk back north along Drottninggatan, and further down and to the left, where one can drive in behind Åhléns, a famous department store, Gunnar's green Volvo 242 is parked in an alley. Robert arrives at the Volvo and has to change into a leather jacket. The boys ask Gunnar where they are going to put the briefcase and he says, "Just throw it in the trunk."

They drive away, turning right and continue on some roads until they come out so that Sveavägen is on the their right side, and see the murder scene from there. From the intersection of Olofsgatan and

34

Tunnelgatan they look to the right and wonder if it is possible to see anything. "Have they come? Oh yes, there seems to be a bit of life in the hatch over there."

Thereafter they turn left and drive over to Tegnergatan where they pick up Thomas H. Thomas says that he had to go out into the street to be able to stop **Leif Ljungqvist** when he arrived with the minivan. They knew he was coming, but Thomas was instructed by Gunnar or Håkan to slow him down somewhat. Otherwise Ljungqvist would have arrived too early at the scene of the murder. Finally, they drive towards the Central Train Station.

# The murder weapon is dumped into a lake

On the night after the murder, the group drove in the green Volvo 242 to Söder Mälarstrand. In the car were Lars M, Rolf K, Jonas N, Håkan E and Thomas H, having picked up Thomas on Tegnergatan. Robert understands that Lars is sitting in the car with the plastic bag with the weapon that he probably received from Rolf.

It was Robert who disposed of the murder weapon, which was in a white plastic bag. Perhaps it ended up approximately 10-15 meters out in the water, Robert thinks. At that time, it was grass and stones occupying the premisses. It has since been converted into a quay and bicycle path. Below the bicycle path there is a small slope with trees, facing down towards the water. So there is a place today that has been located and identified as the place where they stopped and threw in the murder weapon. On the other side of the bay they saw lights from the houses. There and then, Lars stood and discussed what was on the other side of the water.

Furthermore, just after the weapon has been thrown into the water, they drive about 50 meters further away and turn around at a military property, which is still there today but is probably not actively used. This being the same location where Gunnar had previously been and reported his presence and then said to Robert "This is where you sign up before you do anything!".

*During Robert's first interrogation in 1986, he also mentioned where the weapon had been dumped, this being at Söder Mälarstrand. The police then showed Robert a picture of the beach, which they took from an index of cards. The pictures had a checkerboard pattern on them. Robert was asked to point out where he estimated the weapon could be located.*

There's the bright "Hippie bus" with "pink flowers", or similar, waiting for them. It is very unclear what role the "Hippie bus" played, as well as who owned and actually drove the bus. It was an older body-mounted bus, probably of the VW brand, that somehow came to be part of the plot. It was a painted bus with white/pink flowers, it had a smooth black sofa in the front seat, and there were soda crates in the back. It resurfaces several times in Robert's story.

Robert jumps out of the ocean-green Volvo 242 and instead gets into the "Hippie Bus." Then they drove off in that bus. Robert remembers that they drove fast where there was a longer straight stretch towards Slussen, the Locks, and further on past the Viking Line terminal, and continuing further right towards Folkungagatan and then finally onwards Medborgarplatsen.

There they dropped Robert off on the south side of the road that runs before Skanstull. The bus then made a U-turn there and then set off. Then Robert started to walk. He walked along the road on the east side of Skanstull, at times running a bit when he was on the sidewalk. Finally Robert is standing by the stairs at Skanstull. He has a white and red plastic bag in his hand, probably with the bloody rags that he had been given by Rolf to wipe off his blood on after having performed mouth to mouth on Olof Palme. Then he threw the bag in a litter container that was to the left of the stairs. He remembers checking what time it was. It was just after midnight.

During interrogations by the police Robert said that he had sat himself down in the bushes and kind of slept, but that was not true. Instead, he went to the northwest side of the subway, probably the Skanstull station. In addition to this, Robert says that he remembers mentioning that *"it would be a phone call that it had been carried out"*. That is, that the murder had been accomplished. It is not clear to whom the phone call would be placed, nor when this was actually said.

Between 00:30 and 01:00 a.m Robert took the subway to Norsborg. Robert had earlier received SL ticket strips from Gunnar. He thinks he probably got off in Alby, probably he didn't get off at Hallunda station. In Alby, Robert remembers that he was dressed in the very expensive leather jacket that Gunnar had presented him as a gift. Anyway, he put it on prior to the meeting with Håkan, who by then had "taken his jog". A joke that arose from the fact that Håkan was gone for a long time after the murder took place. Following the murder and the reconvening at the bridge, it was proclaimed that Håkan must have "gone for a jog."

Robert walked from Alby station to the road that leads to the parking lot close to Gunnar's building. The purpose of going to Gunnar's place was that Robert had nowhere to sleep at the time. He walked back and forth in the streets. It was too early to wake Gunnar up.

Robert remembers that on the left side, it was around 4 a.m., he met an old lady with a dog. He stopped and talked to her. He doesn't remember what they were talking about. Then he rang Gunnar's front doorbell, even though they had agreed that he would not sleep there then, though Gunnar let him in anyway.

They went into the kitchen, turned on the radio. After half past five in the morning, it was broadcasted on the radio that "Sweden's Prime Minister Olof Palme is dead". Gunnar and Robert didn't say anything to each other then, but instead nodded in agreement. Robert had already understood when they passed by Hötorget that Olof Palme had been murdered by Gunnar, which made him feel disgusted, confused and kind of angry. Also he did not like that they apparently shared money in the car. Robert then went to bed for some sleep. Earlier, Gunnar had said during the night that they won't go into town so very early because it's such a hustle. Robert remembers getting up as early as 8:30 or 9 a.m, proceeding to watching videos, as he often used to do at Gunnar's home.

# Clothing worn around the time of the murder

At the time of the murder, Gunnar was wearing a black coat with wooden buttons, elongated sticks. Robert remembers this because he had to sew in one of the pin buttons that had broken off once. Robert remembers that coat was handed in to a dry cleaner after the murder. The length of that coat was described as "ending above the knees". Gunnar's light jacket, which he changed into immediately after the murder, he had wrapped around himself. He also wore the thin white pants that previously were underneath. Håkan asked "how?", whereupon Gunnar showed and pulled up his dark trousers and showed Håkan, the white thin trousers he wore under the dark trousers.

Håkan had some stubble 4-5 days. He painted his eyebrows dark. But at the time of the murder he had a blue jacket sewn with squares, light worn blue/grey that had pockets on the sides, which was Gunnar's old jacket from the country. Robert believes Håkan was wearing jeans.

Robert himself wore a type of "training jacket, telephone directory blue". The jacket had pockets. It was a so-called "pull on jacket". The trousers were jeans. The jacket was of the type "Adidas fabric", thus not a winter jacket. "My tracksuit jacket was actually a summer jacket. Gunnar tried to wash it as there was blood from Olof Palme on it, but it was not possible to remove, therefor it had to be thrown away", Robert says.

# The day following the murder

Håkan is driving the car and they get off at the intersection of Mäster Samuelsgatan and Slöjdgatan. He parks the car nearby. Robert sees the Hippie Bus parked on Mäster Samuelsgatan, at Åhléns. On the same day, they came to the murder scene and dropped 3 slightly damaged lead bullets there that were narrower than the ones that were actually used.

*To be noted: Up until January 1987 several types of ammunitions were found in the vicinity of the murder scene. This fact caused the lead technician working with the investigation, Wincent Lange, to adopt a very sceptical stance regarding "the official bullets". He stated on several occasions that it is possible the bullets were dropped/planted.*

Rolf boasted in the car and said: "They paid 360,000." But he didn't realise that the others had already spoken to the Skandia men. There was more money in the picture that Rolf did not know about, he had been given his task as an "own" job, as they did not know if they could trust him.

In the evening at Gunnar's house, there was a discussion about Robert's role at the murder scene: "We have to remove Robert from the investigation. This is not possible, we have to do something. We'll have to call Gösta". This probably refers to Gösta Welander, then Deputy County Police Commissioner.

When Håkan sent Robert down to the murder scene, the intention was probably just to get an early report if the assassination attempt had succeeded, but Robert had been involved in attempts to resuscitate him. This created a lot of trouble for Gunnar's gang.

## Handling the LAC tapes

At some point after the murder, probably as soon as Saturday or maybe Sunday at the latest, a tape machine, editing equipment for magnetic tape, arrived at Gunnar's office. Then, according to Robert, Håkan E, who had good experience of editing film etc., should have listened through the LAC tapes and then made the necessary cuts and masks (disturbances) on the tape in question. He said, among other things, that he had accidentally made a cut in the tape at an angle. He asked the others, including Robert, to be quiet so he could hear well and work undisturbed with this.

On Monday morning after the murder at around 9 a.m, after people had gone to work, the professional equipment in terms of clipper 80 X 80 and the tape machine were prepared, they were silver in colour. Gunnar didn't want to rent a trailer but his good friend **Håkan B** could help to get a private trailer. With a car and trailer, you covered the equipment with some kind of tarpaulin on the trailer. In discussions with Håkan B in the autumn of 2023, Håkan B has confirmed that he conveyed a trailer for Gunnar. Håkan, as an experienced radio amateur, was also a knowledgeable advisor when it came to eavesdropping and radio communication via walkie-talkie. Incidentally, Håkan felt that he had not been particularly involved in Gunnar's project. Police officer G, possibly named Göran, was supposed to have the LAC tapes back by Monday morning immediately after the murder.

## The trip to Idre

Gunnar and Robert had skied together on several occasions before, including in Sälen. Skies and skiing boots were purchased for the previous trips in Täby Centrum, north of Stockholm.

A few days after the murder, Robert, Gunnar and a few others again were in the green Volvo, driving up to Stig Engström in Idre to ski together. Robert didn't know in advance that Stig would be there, but he was anyway allowed into Stig's cabin. He remembers that it was cosy, and that Stig's wife also was there. Robert also remembers in particular what it looked like in the toilet, because Gunnar demonstrated that there was a hatch where objects could be concealed. There is a memory of placing a key above the garbage container.

As far as Robert remembers, Gunnar and Robert had their own cottage, located about 700 meters from Stig's. Stig came to Gunnar's office before he went to Idre. On Wednesday or Thursday they set off to Idre.

Gunnar and Stig spoke, but Robert was then allowed to go out and has not picked up anything about what was said then. Robert believes that the gang went skiing and Robert met Stig on one occasion on the slopes. Robert mostly skied by himself.

Robert has said the following: "We didn't know if we could go up to Idre on the Wednesday or Thursday after the murder, depending on how much that had to be arranged. Among other things, they wanted to know what was in the newspapers in the days after the murder."

On the way home from Idre, Gunnar called Joel Ö and was worried about which route they should take back to Stockholm, probably he did not want to be checked by the police.

# The trip to Lanzarote

Robert doesn't know exactly when they went to Lanzarote, one of the Canary Islands, but it was winter in Sweden so it can't be that long after the murder. There are pictures from there and a lot to tell.

Robert and Gunnar flew from Arlanda to Lanzarote and stayed for about two weeks. They lived in the southern part, more specifically in Puerto del Carmen. Nearby there was an old, abandoned neighbourhood where Gunnar, Robert and possibly other people were set to meet a person unknown to Robert. So Gunnar was looking for someone who lived there and who he needed to get in touch with. It seemed that it was a pre-arranged meeting, but the purpose of the meeting is unknown to Robert.

On the second day, **Jonas N** arrived with his girlfriend. They stayed in a luxury hotel. They met Jonas. On the third day, they visited a sailboat marina on the north side of the island. Together they went out with a dinghy from a beach. Afterwards Jonas flew with his girlfriend to Mallorca. From there they sailed with their own sailboat from Mallorca to Lanzarote. Jonas's sister or brother was also along on the trip to Lanzarote. Jonas and his wife sailed from Lanzarote to the United States, across the Atlantic, immediately after their visit there. This according to Robert. Robert has visited the Canary Islands on subsequent occasions, twice he believes, in addition to this trip in 1986, but then with his family. Robert has admitted that he may have mixed up some details with trips that took place later on.

# Visit to Stig Engström's office

Sometime after the murder, Robert remembers that Gunnar dropped Robert off at Stig Engström's office in the Skandia building. Robert then asked, "What am I supposed to do here?"
"You can go up to Stig. While I attend to other matters."

Robert remembers his office in detail. You could walk through the office. You came in to the right at the window turned left towards the property to the east. One more door, then a toilet, "sophisticated furnished room". There was a darkroom for developing photographs. Robert was standing in the darkroom with Stig. Robert thought it was a bit weird and got an uneasy feeling and wondered if Stig would do something with Robert, but nothing happened.

# Gunnar Ställfors has a meeting with the police

Sometime after Palme's murder, Gunnar Ställfors and Robert drove into town late in the evening where they were to have a meeting with the police. Robert thinks it was night, maybe at around 11 p.m. Robert is unsure when it was, it might even have been weeks or months after Idre, but still believes that this brief meeting was very soon after the murder.

Robert says he perceives the meeting as some kind of "final report of the murder". They came by car, perhaps from the north side. Gunnar thought about where to park his green Volvo so as not to draw unnecessary attention to himself – "maybe because he was afraid that someone would take photos of this meeting," Robert says.

At first, Robert says that he thinks they parked "20 meters behind a Volvo 242, a black and white police vehicle". "We parked the car more to the south before the pillar". A few days later, he corrects himself and says that they probably parked on the other side of the road and walked over to the murder scene. However, Robert is unsure where they actually parked.

Once in place, Robert is directed to stand behind the police car, by the tailgate, whereafter Gunnar says, "Wait here for now!"
Gunnar then walks over to the grey round pillar that is right at the subway entrance where he meets up with a uniformed policeman, "It was an older policeman, maybe in his 50's. He wore a classic black leather jacket that the police wore at the time." Maybe there was another guy at the scene. Robert says in a later conversation that he thinks there were probably several police officers on site and that he remembers the pile of flowers.

***To be noted.*** *Robert recalling the pile of flowers still being in place supports his recollection that the meeting with the police officers occurred early on after the murder. The bed of flowers were removed sometime in March 1986.*

After Gunnar and the police had conversed for a short while, Robert remembers that the policeman then walks up to Robert who is standing behind the police car. There he is asked to show identification, which he does. Robert believes he identified himself with a personal subway card that he had. Then the policeman says, "Now you can leave!" which Gunnar and Robert subsequently did.

Robert later stated that he might even have been at the pillar and spoke to the policeman and explained what he had been through in connection with the murder: "The idea was that we finally reported the murder."

There were maybe 4-5 people nearby at the murder scene. The police car was on the pavement.

Robert notices that Gunnar becomes more reserved towards him in 1986 but it is difficult to say in retrospect when this attitude change begins[8].


## Gunnar Ställfors meets Mårten Palme

Robert says that "Mårten Palme and Gunnar Ställfors, who shot his father, met in a café in Stockholm not many days after the murder. They drove in the direction of Gärdet and then to an area called "Fältöversten". It was located in the north of Stockholm. Gunnar had said before: "I have to talk to him."

It was Håkan E who arranged the meeting between the two through some contact he had. Robert was in the office when he first heard that this was going to be arranged.

"Can't we meet Mårten Palme at the bookstore?" he asked. Robert accompanied Gunnar in his car. They parked on the right side of the road. Robert had to stay in the car all the time and never saw Mårten Palme in person. The meeting between Gunnar and Mårten lasted about 20-30 minutes, Robert estimates[9].

# Final words to reflect upon

Robert has on several occasions provided information regarding the murder of Palme to the police, the most recent occasion being in April 2018. Citizens have the right to obtain their own interrogation material, as well as other information they have provided to the ongoing investigation. Thus Robert has requested these but the results regarding the year 2018 were meagre. Because of this Robert sent the following question to Sven-Åke Blombergsson, who was actively working with the case up til the year 2020:

From: robert barestrand <******@*****>
Sent: den 22 April 2024 15:05
To: Sven Åke Blombergsson
<sven-ake.blombergsson@polisen.se> Subject: Lack of interrogations....

This is a message from an external sender. Don't open links and attachments if you're unsure of the content.

Regarding tips about the Palme murder

Hi Sven-Åke Blombergsson,

My name is Robert Barestrand, 691112-****, and I visited you in April 2018 at the police station on Kungsholmen and then left a tip about the Palme murder. The  last winter we talked on the phone and then you remembered that I had been visiting and that I came in my work clothes. My memory is that in April 2018, after the meeting, I had to sign an interrogation. Now I have requested all my tips and interrogations regarding the murder of Olof Palme and even though an extended search has been made, my interrogation with you is not included in the result. I do not understand this, have you forgotten to register the interrogation or has it ended up on some other identity.?? What explanation do you have.

Best regards Robert Barestrand

The following reply were received:

From: sven-ake.blombergsson@polisen.se <sven-ake.blombergsson@polisen.se>
Date: mån 22 apr. 2024 15:29
Subject: SV: Missing Interrogations....

To: robert barestrand <******@*****>
Hi Robert,

I just replied to a text message to your friend O*****

I remember that you were visiting in April 2018 and it was the 5th at 13.00 which I wrote down in my diary that I still have today. On the text message to O***** just now, I wrote the 18th, which is wrong.

Unfortunately, I cannot give a good explanation for this, which I also stated on the phone earlier. What I do know is that you have NOT signed any interrogation because that is not the routine. Had it been an interrogation, it would have been registered. The most likely thing is that you left a tip, which I also wrote down in my diary when we booked the appointment in 2018.

I do not remember today exactly what the tip was about but the information that has come to light in the present from you regarding a form of confusion which is new to both me and Peter Steude.

It is likely that you left an anonymous tip without name and social security number containing information that does not match what has come to light at the present. It can be ruled out that it has ended up "on some other identity" as you wrote.

Kindly,

Sven-Åke Blombergsson


--------------------------


What can be said about this? Here is an investigator belonging to the Palme Group sitting with an informant at a planned meeting, whom apparently is known by name, and that information provided including several names is not registered either on Robert B or, hence, even anonymously. We have requested to receive all anonymous tips registered on April 5, 2018, and none of them appear to exist.

If the police neglect to register some information that is supplied to a murder investigation, as in this case, then they can end up with completely wrongly drawn conclusions, just as they have done in this case. Stig Engström was not a murderer, but he participated in a conspiracy against Prime Minister Olof Palme.

It's up to now only Robert Barestrand who has tried to inform the police about this matter.

# Appendices – testimonies from the investigation

That which follows is actual transcriptions of original interrogations performed by the Swedish Police. However, it should be noted that clarifying editing has been applied for enhanced readability as well as coherency but we at the same time wish to emphasise that the core content has by no means been altered in any sense. Original testimonies are available at the following websites:

www.itdemokrati.nu

www.wpu.nu

palmemordsarkivet.se

Hence the review will contain interrogations of those who can be considered most relevant to Robert's statements. Perhaps Mrs. Anna Hage is the best source for this venture, therefore her statements will accordingly be presented first.

*According to statements in Anna Hages second interrogation, where the term "stripling" first surfaces:*

## "Furthermore, there was a stripling who was dwelling by the man's head."

Most people tend to know that Stefan Glantz tried to save Olof Palme by applying the mouth-to-mouth method and therefore they subsequently have believed that Stefan G was the "stripling". If such were the case, it means that Stefan would have arrived first at the scene of the murder, even before Anna H, which is completely unreasonable if one reads Lena Bäsen's, Göran Israelsson's and Stefan's own interrogations.

Lena Bäsen shared a taxi with Stefan, she says that she and four friends had had dinner at Lilla Köpenhamn and that they thereafter had tried to get into the Union but one boy was denied access and thus was making his way home instead. Lena, together with the others, Stefan G, Göran I and Kennet E then took a taxi to the institution Albatross. Lena sat in the front and the boys sat in the back. She didn't see anything special until they came up to Tunnelgatan. **Suddenly, she saw a man lying on the sidewalk.** Her immediate thought was that it was the friend they had lost earlier in the evening. She exclaimed this so that the driver could hear it.

*"As soon as the taxi stopped, Bäsen jumped out of the car and ran up to the lying man. At the same time, another woman who she later found out is called Anne, and a man in a gray jacket came forward".*

Apparently Lena Bäsen does not recognise "the man in the gray jacket", she does however recognise Stefan G, who arrived with the same taxi. We believe that the "man in the gray jacket" is a hitherto unidentified man who was first to arrive to Lisbeth Palme and assisted her in turning Olof around a bit and possibly tried resuscitation, whereas he became bloody around the mouth.

"Bäsen was asked if she had heard anyone mention where the perpetrator had gone. Bäsen then remembers that the man with the gray jacket had mentioned something about "he took that way". At that point, we turned towards the alley, i.e. Tunnelgatan to the east. The man in the gray jacket had been about Bäsen's own age. He was fair-haired."

Stefan G has, according to his own information, not seen any fleeing person whatsoever.

"Stefan G further says that during the journey or, for that matter, in connection with the stop, **he did not see anything that could benefit the investigation."**

In addition, Stefan says that when he arrived **"to the man lying on his back"**, i.e, this means somebody had already turned Olof Palme around at this point in time.

On the 2nd of March, Anna Hage was interviewed by Länstidningen in Södertälje and the young man was still present in her story: *"A woman and a stripling crouched over him and I understood that something had happened very recently."*

In Anna Hage's 3rd interrogation on April the 2nd, 1986, i.e. about one month later, the stripling had been omitted from her narrative. Before the district court, Anna H claims that she was the first to arrive at the scene of the murder and that Stefan G arrived later. This is essentially correct, although no one asks her why the stripling that was present in her early narratives now had been omitted.

On 25/4/1988 Anna Hage is with the police and by her own request gets to read all of her interrogations. After the reading is completed she does not want to change or supplement anything.

Anna Hage once received  what can be interpreted as a warning from a uniformed military man during an agreed meeting at Stora Konditoriet, Södertälje, in August 1988. In Mrs. Hage's own book, "30 years of silence", she writes that the unknown uniformed man proclaimed:

*"It is very important that there is no focus on the wrong things. Some things shouldn't come out."*

*To be noted: Information about who this person was has been revealed by documents made public after the closure of the pre-investigation in 2020. The person in question figures in the investigation under the pseudonym "Private investigator Mats". Although his motives for courting Mrs. Hage are unclear, the episode is worth mentioning in the light of Mrs. Hage's statements in her own book.*

**Reference number**: E-19
**Data recipients:** Detective Inspector E. Näslund
**Date:** 1/3/1986
**Time:** 00.15 a.m.
**Crime with which the spread is connected**: The murder of Olof Palme
**Informant:** Anna Birgitta, Hage
**Date of birth:** 11/9/1968
**Address:** Torsgatan 4,151 36 Södertälje,tfn 0755-855 60
**Place of work:** Student, Tälje High School, Nursing program

**Miss Hage states**: On Friday the 28th of February 1986 she and her friend Karin Johansson had visited Filmstaden (A cinema) at Mäster Samuelsgatan. They left Filmstaden around 23 o clock and then they met up with three friends going by car, at Norrlandsgatan. They drove from Norrlandsgatan to Sveavägen and passed Kungsgatan in the left lane.

**Just after they passed Kungsgatan she saw a man lying on the right (east) side on the pathway of Sveavägen. She was under the impression that the man might have had a hearth attack or an epileptic seizure and the car was stopped and she ran to the man.** At the same time she noticed a man that was about ten meters away from the lying man. She perceived this man - X - as being middle-aged, dark and wearing a 3/4 length coat or jacket. She doesn't think he had anything in his hands. X disappeared into a side street on the right.

**When she came up to the man who was lying on the walkway she saw that he was bleeding from the mouth and the nose. A woman stood next to the man and a man -Y- was crouched down by the injured mans head.** She felt if the injured man - Z- had a pulse and therefore first felt his neck and thereafter the wrist. She did not feel any pulse. She turned -Z- on his back and gave him two heart spurts, then continued with compressions - about- 10-20 times. **Y gave Z artificial respiration by blowing in air a couple of times.** The woman next to A seemed to be shocked and pushed miss Hage away and yelled that an ambulance would come and that doctors would perform surgery.

An ambulance arrived at the scene and at about the same time police personnel arrived. In her opinion -Z- appeared lifeless and had rigid eyes. She did not recognise the man but later found out that Z was Prime Minister Olof Palme. The woman later presented herself as being Mrs. Palme.

Miss Hage can not give any specific description of the man X. It was quite dark in the surroundings. Her focus was to get Z s heart rate going if possible as Z in her opinion was deeply unconscious.

Read aloud as go.

The interrogation ended 01.05 a.m.

**Reference number:** E-19-A
**Data recipients:** Detective Inspector Åke Torstensson
**Date:** 3/3/1986
**Time:** 5.45 p.m.
**Crime with which the spread is connected:** The murder of Olof Palme
**Informant:** Anna Birgitta, Hage
**Date of birth:** 11/9/1968
**Address:** Torsgatan 4,151 36 Södertälje,tfn 0755-855 60
**Place of work:** Student, Tälje High School, Nursing program
**Action:** Follow up by Tip E-19

**Story:** Anna perceived the running man as middle-aged and of middle-height. He seemed broad-shouldered and his head seemed too small in relation to his body. She did not see the man s hands and therefore can t say if he was carrying anything. Because he was running with the kiosk-like square as a backdrop, Anna perceived him as dark - dark coat and dark hair. As for the attire she is pretty sure that the man wore a 3/4 long coat. She substantiates this by stating that she saw the light between his calves but not between his thighs when he ran. She believes that if he had been wearing a short coat, she should have seen the light between his legs all the way up to his crotch when he ran. She made no observation on any footwear. She perceived him as bareheaded. Anna judged that the man was running in a straight line from the lying man. She does not think that he d come running round a corner for example, because he would have had a different location in the street. She is very unsure but believes that the man ran to the left of the kiosk- like square.
**When Anna got out of the car, she also saw a woman**

**standing next to the man laying down. Further there was
a youth that dwelt by the mans head. The two observed
were fiddling with the man that was laying down. The
youth at the reclining mans head was dressed in a
medium blue waist jacket, a sweater and jeans. He had a
narrow face and was dark-haired.**

The woman next to the man lying down, was very talkative
but Anna does not remember what she said.
Anna has not been at the scene since the incident described
above. Regarding Anna s observation of the injured man and
her remedial measures, reference is made to previous
interrogation.

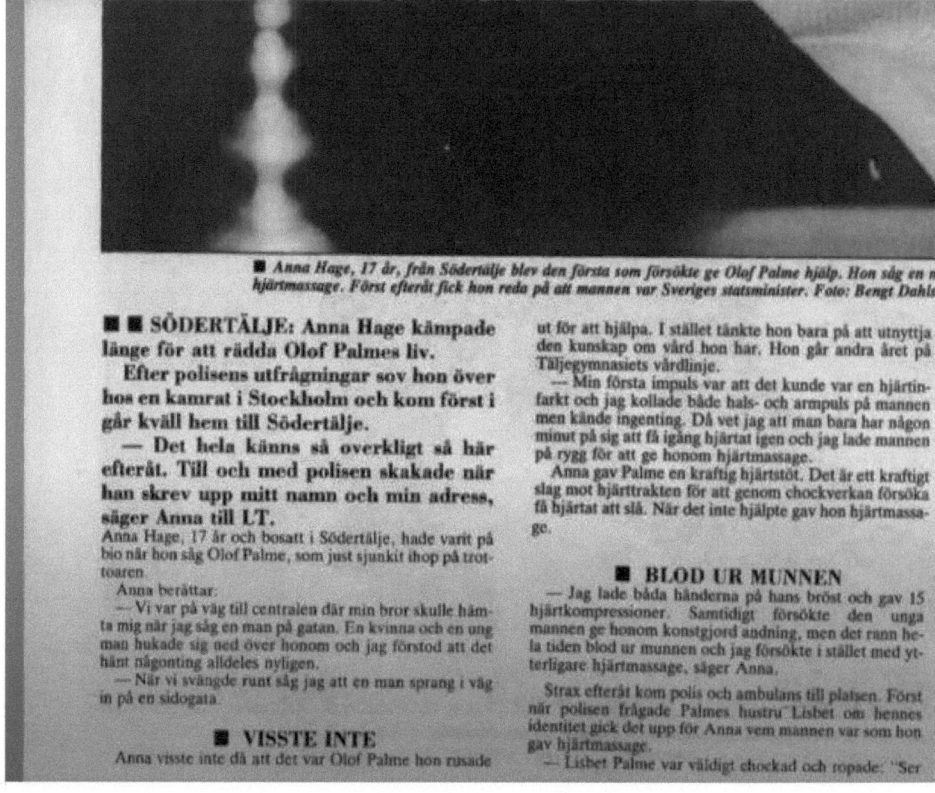

■ *Anna Hage, 17 år, från Södertälje blev den första som försökte ge Olof Palme hjälp. Hon såg en ma* *hjärtmassage. Först efteråt fick hon reda på att mannen var Sveriges statsminister. Foto: Bengt Dahlste*

■ ■ **SÖDERTÄLJE: Anna Hage kämpade länge för att rädda Olof Palmes liv.**

Efter polisens utfrågningar sov hon över hos en kamrat i Stockholm och kom först i går kväll hem till Södertälje.

— Det hela känns så overkligt så här efteråt. Till och med polisen skakade när han skrev upp mitt namn och min adress, säger Anna till LT.

Anna Hage, 17 år och bosatt i Södertälje, hade varit på bio när hon såg Olof Palme, som just sjunkit ihop på trottoaren.

Anna berättar:

— Vi var på väg till centralen där min bror skulle hämta mig när jag såg en man på gatan. En kvinna och en ung man hukade sig ned över honom och jag förstod att det hänt någonting alldeles nyligen.

— När vi svängde runt såg jag att en man sprang i väg in på en sidogata.

■ **VISSTE INTE**

Anna visste inte då att det var Olof Palme hon rusade ut för att hjälpa. I stället tänkte hon bara på att utnyttja den kunskap om vård hon har. Hon går andra året på Täljegymnasiets vårdlinje.

— Min första impuls var att det kunde var en hjärtinfarkt och jag kollade både hals- och armpuls på mannen men kände ingenting. Då vet jag att man bara har någon minut på sig att få igång hjärtat igen och jag lade mannen på rygg för att ge honom hjärtmassage.

Anna gav Palme en kraftig hjärtstöt. Det är ett kraftigt slag mot hjärttrakten för att genom chockverkan försöka få hjärtat att slå. När det inte hjälpte gav hon hjärtmassage.

■ **BLOD UR MUNNEN**

— Jag lade båda händerna på hans bröst och gav 15 hjärtkompressioner. Samtidigt försökte den unga mannen ge honom konstgjord andning, men det rann hela tiden blod ur munnen och jag försökte i stället med ytterligare hjärtmassage, säger Anna.

Strax efteråt kom polis och ambulans till platsen. Först när polisen frågade Palmes hustru Lisbet om hennes identitet gick det upp för Anna vem mannen var som hon gav hjärtmassage.

— Lisbet Palme var väldigt chockad och ropade: "Ser

SÖDERTÄLJE: Anna Hage fought to save Olof Palme's life.

After being questioned by police during the late hours, she slept over at a friend's house in Stockholm and only arrived home to Södertälje last night.
- It all feels so unreal afterwards. Even the police was shaken when he wrote down my name and address, Anna says to LT. Anna Hage, 17 years old and living in Södertälje, had

been at the cinema when she saw Olof Palme, who had just collapsed on the pavement.

Anna recalls:
"We were on our way to the Central Station where my brother was going to pick me up when I saw a man lying on the street. **A woman and a young man were crouched over him and I understood that something had happened very recently.**

"When we turned around, I saw that a man ran away into a side street.”

## Anna Hage in the district court, June 1989

*H = Hage*
*Pro H = Prosecutor Helin*

H: Umm

Pro H: "When she came up to the man that was lying on the sidewalk she saw that he was bleeding from the mouth and the nose. A woman stood next to the man and **a man - Y - was crouched down by the injured mans head" It's a little different from what you said today** because you said that you were the first that came up to Olof Palme and after a while someone else came up and asked if he could help.

H: Yes.

Pro H: What about that?

H: No, I arrived first.

Pro H: You were first.

H: Stefan Glans came just..just after.

Pro H: Umm. Then two days later you were interrogated, the 3d of mars, do you remember that interrogation?.......

*Interrogation Karin Johansson no 2, 2/4/1986 at 15.10 p.m.*

*J= Johansson*
*I= Interrogator*

J: I think that, it looks like an old couple, and I probably thought the man had had a heart attack or something like that. My first thought was that, help, there are no people here, maybe I can help with something. Since I'm a scout I have, first aid I know. In any case, you can call an ambulance and calm her down.

I: But as far as you remember ......

J: Then Anna said to me, come on we have to help. Like, I had just thought about it and kind of hadn't had time to say anything.

I: But as far as you can see now, you see a man lying on the ground and a woman by his side?

J: Yes.

I: No other person around?

**J: That's what I can't connect if I see Stefan directly or, I don't think I saw him directly.**

I: Did you see any, it's this Stefan?

J: Yes I think so, no one else, not that I have noticed anyway.

I: Anna apparently jumps out of the car first?

59

J: Yes, she sits closest.

I: And you right after her?

J: Yes.

I: Can you describe what you do?

J: We run up to the man and the woman, then Stefan has arrived. They have put him in a forward prone side position.

I: Who has done it?

J: Stefan, yes Stefan has done it I think it was, help with Lisbeth then maybe, I don't know. Anna since she knows heart massage, she and Stefan help each other and try resuscitation attempts while I try to calm Lisbeth down. Lisbeth tries to pull away, she pulled Anna away, slapped her and said that there would be a doctor for it.

I: What kind of comment is made?

J: A comment is made that, by Lisbeth or by the public?

I: From Lisbeth.

J: That there should be a doctor for this.

**Page 2:**

…this so that the driver could hear it. This may have caused the driver to react extra quickly, and thus made a so-called U-turn and turned up on the curb near the lying man. When Bäsen first noticed the man, she can't remember seeing any other people around except the woman who was bent over the man. When asked, she states that she has not seen any man on his way away from the scene.

**As soon as the taxi stopped, Bäsen jumped out of the car and ran up to the lying man. At the same time, another woman who she later found out was named Anne, as well as a man in a grey jacket came forward.** At first, Bäsen had thought that the man had collapsed due to illness, but when she arrived, she saw how the blood pulsing and understood that he had been shot. She thought the whole thing was very unpleasant, and she felt that she could not look any further, so she walked away towards the front of the building and thus turned her back to the lying person. She squatted there to try to recover. She almost regurgitated from what she had seen. While she was sitting there, Kenneth Ersson came up and tried to comfort her. Bäsen had seen that a police picket had arrived at the scene, other than that, she did not make many observations because she always had her face to the front of the building and her back turned away from the events.

When asked, Bäsen states that she did not notice any more people other than **just Anne and the person in the gray jacket.** Of course, there are many more people at the scene, but there were none that Bäsen could recall. Bäsen was asked if she had seen anyone with a blue jacket, but she says she has no such memory. When asked if she saw any middle-aged man with glasses, a cap and a long coat, she also states that she has no memory of any such man. When asked, she also states that she has not seen any person further up the alley towards Luntmakargatan. She points out again that she had her face turned towards the front of the building and therefore did not have the opportunity to make any further observations.

After the ambulance picked up the wounded man, there was, according to Bäsen, a general chaos at the scene, but Bäsen and the....

**Page 3:**

Others who had arrived in the taxi gathered themselves and got back in the taxi, after which they left the scene. Bäsen had not stated her name to the police. They then went onto restaurant Albatross as they had previously decided.

The taxi that Bäsen was riding in was a white Mercedes or Volvo. She never found out the driver's name.

Bäsen was asked if she had heard that the woman next to the fallen man, i.e. Lisbeth Palme, had said anything. Bäsen states that she heard that Lisbeth said something, but not what. She had been upset and Bäsen got the impression that she got the driver who had driven Bäsen's taxi to call an ambulance. She hadn't heard Lisbeth say anything about the perpetrator.

Bäsen was asked if she had heard anyone mention where the perpetrator had gone. Bäsen then wants to remember that the man with the grey jacket had mentioned something about "that he had taken that way". At this point, pointing towards the alley, i.e. Tunnelgatan to the east. The man in the gray jacket had been about Bäsen's own age. The man was fair-haired.

*I = Interrogator, B= Bäsen*

I: Yes Lena now you have listened when I read this. Is it correctly understood by me?

B: Yes it is.

I: Do you have anything you would like to add that I have not asked you here?

B: No, not that I can think of now.

I: Then the interrogation ends at 09.09 a.m.

Stockholm as above
Paul Johansson Detective Inspector

## Interrogation Stefan Glantz 5/3/1986 at 18.00 p.m.

**Reference number:** E9979-3
**Data recipients:** A. Bäckström Date: 5/3/1986
**Time:** 6.00 p.m.
**Crime with which the spread is connected:** The murder of Olof Palme
**Informant:** Nils Stefan, Glantz
**Date of birth:** 16/7/1963
**Address:** Trevebovägen 36,184 00 Åkersberga,tfn 0764-618 36
**Profession:** Student
**Place of work:** STI, Bältgatan Klass 4 HV Building Construction Technology
**Action:** Area 1

## Facts:

Glanz states that on Friday 28/2 1986 during the evening he stayed at the student union behind McDonalds on Sveavägen together with Göran Israelsson together with a girl with an unknown name and living in Stockholm, a friend of Israelsson's. At about 11 p.m., they took a taxi for a ride to Kungsgatan. **As far as he remembers, they stopped for a red light and the taxi driver saw a man lying down and made a u-turn at Tunnelgatan so that he came close to the lying man.** They all jumped out and Israelsson rushed up to the man lying on his back. He cannot say which way his head was pointing. He turned the man with the help of others in a forward prone side position and took his pulse. He felt it faintly. He saw that there was too much blood running around his mouth and managed to get this out **and started the mouth-to-mouth method. At the same time, a girl, later identified as Anna Hage, had arrived at the scene and started CPR.** They were doing this for what

Glans estimates about 2 minutes, after which an ambulance arrived at the scene that took Palme away.

He further says that during the journey there or in connection with the stop, he did not see anything that could benefit the investigation. He has also discussed with his comrades and none of them have said that they have noticed anything that can be linked to the crime. **During the interrogation, the telephone number is given to Anna Hage at her request.**

# Interrogation Göran Israelsson, 3/2/1988 at 15.35 p.m.

**Reference number:** E9979-7-A
**Data recipients:** Ingvar Kjellvås
**Date:** 3/2/1988
**Time:** 3.35 p.m.
**Crime with which the spread is connected:** The murder of Olof Palme
**The reconnaissance spread has been submitted:** By phone
**Informant:** Göran Israelsson
**Date of Birth:** 23/6/1962
**Address:** Trevebovägen 26,184 00 Åkersberga,tfn 0764-23350
**Place of work:** Phone 0764-660 00
**Action:** Follow up by E-17 tip

## Facts:

A short time before the murder occurred, he took a taxi from the institution Glädjehuset with Stefan Glanz, Kennet Ersson and Lena Bäsen. They drove Sveavägen south, he sat on the front right on the passenger side.
The taxi stopped at the intersection of Sveavägen - Tunnelgatan and they stood as the first car, in which lane they were he does not remember.

When they were sitting in the car, someone looked to the left and saw how a person was lying on the sidewalk, Göran then looked to the left and saw how a person was lying on the sidewalk, around were 3 - 4 people.

He did not see any person running from the scene. He also did not hear any shots or see any person firing any weapon. After about 15 seconds it turned green and the taxi made a U-turn and parked next to the sidewalk at the murder scene.

No other car was then nearby, that he noticed. As he understood it, they arrived as the first car.

Göran cannot describe the people who were standing around the person lying on the sidewalk, but it was the same people who were still standing when they arrived. **He can only say that it was a lady and a guy. The guy had apparently made resuscitation attempts because he was all bloody around the mouth.**

**When he arrived at the scene, two more girls arrived who also helped with resuscitation attempts on the injured man. The guy who was bloody in the face told me that a man had run from the scene.**

Göran then looked up Tunnelgatan east towards Malmskillnadsgatan but he didn't see any person in the alley/street.
More people arrived at the scene and a greater confusion arose.
After 5-10 minutes, the first police car arrived at the scene. Göran had then taken of his friend Lena Bäsen, who had become nauseous from the incident.

Göran states that he has previously been questioned by the police.

The interrogation ends at 3.55 p.m.


/Ingvar Kjellvås Detective Inspector/

# Footnotes

[1] **Gunnar Ställfors**, born 19/9/1934, dead 1/10/2015. Perpetrator, entertainment organiser. Since 1988 mainly resident in Sri Lanka.

[2] **Bertil Albons**, Åke Sven Bertil, born 6/10/1939, deceased 9/4/2011. Former bank director at SEB.

[3] **Stig Engström**, Stig Folke Wilhem, born 26/2/1934 in Calcutta, India. Deceased 10/6/2000.

[4] **Ann-Kristin Magnusson**/Bonnier/Wallenberg, born 3/4/1951. Perished 2019 in a sailing accident in Switzerland.

[5] This could possibly have been **Nicola Fauzzi**, the chef who later met the Palme couple at La Carterie. Robert says he remembers him because he was modern equipped with NIKE backpack and headphones.

[6] There are witness reports that 2 men run up the stairs towards Malmskillnadsgatan, see analysis (in Swedish):
https://efolket.eu/mordet-pa-olof-palme-det-forsvunna-garningsmannavittnet-pa-tunnelgatan/

[7] **Stig Engström** has, according to Robert, run Tunnelgatan east at a very early stage when there were no police to try to catch up with. The story of the police chase is therefore probably a fabrication.

[8] This strange incident can be interpreted as someone in the police, with knowledge of Robert's first contact with the police, contacts Gunnar and tells him that Robert has been "gossiping". Gunnar then says that Robert has vivid fantasies. The meeting is supposed to scare Robert into silence, he won't dare to go to the police again.

[9] The probable motive for Gunnar to meet with Mårten Palme was to scare the Palme family into passivity during the murder investigation. In the group around Gunnar, there were several malicious rumours about Olof Palme, which were also used internally to justify the murder.

# The Ferry disaster revisited

# The Sinking of the M/V Estonia

# The Estonia catastrophe, a prelude

As citizens of recognised democracies it is hard to grasp that leaders of such nations would resort to unconventional measures to, as will be shown, present a fabricated explanation to a disaster that affected thousands of people directly and, therefore, indirectly thousands upon thousands in the aftermath. Questions arose immediately what could have caused the catastrophic sinking. And, furthermore, why the initial answers never convinced those who looked deeper into the fatality. The aforementioned were also in several cases shunned and ostracised, paving the way for an acceptable explanation. As will be shown further on this acceptable explanation is severely flawed in several instances.

# The initial reactions

The then outgoing prime minister of Sweden, Carl Bildt, announced on the following morning that the root cause for the sinking was the failure of the bow visor. A bold proclamation from somebody who had probably never even seen one in action in real life. Surviving third engineer on duty, **Margus Treu**, on the other hand, proclaimed that there was "water up to our knees in the engine room". And, furthermore, he gave an even more important statement; "the bilge pumps were running". This has been completely neglected by the official investigation. These statements, as will be explained further on, are incompatible with the official narrative. Thus, as early as in the morning following the event, there were two versions of the chain of events available. One from a politician, the second from an engineer who survived the casualty.

It is furthermore to be noted that the date in question, the 28th of September, was also the day the newly elected government of Sweden came into power.

And as an additional note, it was also decided during this date to set up a commission to oversee the investigation of the Murder of Olof Palme. This can be considered as a mere coincidence and demands no further analysis, other than that an equivalent should have been established regarding the J.A.I.C. and its utter failure and the consequences thereof.

## The J.A.I.C.

The Joint Accident Investigating Commission was erected to work broadly and internationally. In all senses it failed. Even minor or close call incidents always result in a trial in court, commonly referred to as "Sea Trials". But a disaster of unheard magnitude does not, this according to the logic of the J.A.I.C. This is unique in the history of shipping, there are no known accidents at sea that have not ended up in a court of law. Furthermore, as will be shown, the J.A.I.C. neglected to perform interrogations based on the rule of law. Very few properly conducted interrogations are available, except those emanating from the Estonian side who directly decided to treat the case as a criminal investigation.

The Swedish side, on the contrary, let interrogators sit with the official theory smacked open in a double page in the face of the survivor being questioned, an obvious coercion on the part of the J.A.I.C. Any witness or survivor should always be free to describe their experience as it was, without external interference. This was blatantly ignored from the Swedish side who instead seemed to intentionally divert from this practice.

Thankfully, as mentioned earlier, the Estonian side treated it as a criminal case, and therefore provided both professional interrogators and supporting individuals for the witnesses, as well as making the statements available to marine experts. It is from these procedures the most valuable and unaffected statements can be found.

The extracted official sequence of events and timeline depict a flooded car deck due to the loss of the bow visor, which was also supposed to have torn open the forward ramp, thus exposing the car deck to the open sea.

# The myths

Several easily falsified myths were quickly established to support the official narrative. Of course this indeed should immediately have raised concerns and alarm, as clear warning signs that something out of the ordinary was going on. The rapid spreading of the myths mainly via the media contributed to derailing any dispassionate discussion and analysis.

## *Harsh weather*

The average wind speed at the time of the casualty was approximately 17 m/s. That is in no way to be considered as extreme or constitute speculations of irresponsible handling of the vessel. It was during the aftermath that harsh winds started to occur, during the rescue operations the average wind speed rose to around 21 m/s. When the actual casualty happened, the weather and hight of the waves can be considered usual, slight to medium, rough conditions. Nothing significant in relation to the vessel itself and the effect on it can be derived from the weather conditions. On the contrary, according to SMHI, even during the rescue operations neither wind speeds or wave heights constituted the definition of a storm. The real, and thus not particularly severe conditions, were described as gale force winds with rising wave heights in the morning. During the casualty of M/V Estonia, it can consequently be concluded that no exceptional weather conditions were present at the time of the casualty.

## *Classification society*

One of the most ridiculous ideas brought forward is that the vessel was not cleared for its route and therefore was operated in breach of restrictions. And what is worse, as even "experts" proclaim, that it is the reason for the disaster.

The M/V Viking Sally, later renamed M/V Estonia, was built and completed in Mayer Werft, West Germany, in the year of 1979. There exists no documentation that the ferries route should be restricted. The construction was similar or identical to that of all then current operating ferries in the Baltic Sea, regardless of route. In particular Viking Line had the habit of rearranging its vessel's routes. By that it is highly unlikely there were ever any restrictions imposed whatsoever.

These speculations can simply be put down to ignorance in combination with a desire to satisfy the yearning public, as well as striving to portrait the vessel as unseaworthy.

If that were the case several subsequent owners should thereby also be complicit, if the Swedes' logic is to be applied that is. The Finnish Maritime Administration granted the ferry in question a licence to operate between Umeå and Vaasa before it was sold to Estline. The Wasa King, as it was subsequently renamed, received clearance from the classification society for the intended route. In the seas in question heavy weather is common and occasionally constitutes delays to the operating vessels, nowadays even inhibiting voyages completely.

The conclusions are therefore, that the ferry in question, was duly fit for its intended route between Stockholm and Tallinn. Nothing has ever been put forward to indicate the contrary.

## *Handling of the vessel*

Another famous myth is that the crew on the bridge were retaining a speed of the vessel not suitable for the weather conditions. Here once again complete ignorance surfaces. At the time of the casualty, as has already been shown, the weather conditions were not exceptionally harsh, thus any reduction of speed would have lacked any purpose. Since no grounds existed for a reduction in speed it was not even to be considered under the circumstances prevailing at the time.

Very few vessels would arrive on time if a reduction in speed was applied for similar conditions that the M/V Estonia encountered. On the contrary, even to this day, captains regularly force their ships up to maximum effect just for the sake that the time of arrival will not be delayed for all too long. Engine output is not to be confused with actual speed of a vessel. It is not even possible for a ferry, in harsh conditions, to maintain such a speed that could constitute a risk to the integrity of the vessel.

## *Supposed incompetence*

This appalling attack on the crew of the M/V Estonia can easily be dismissed by statements from surveyors of the M/V Estonia. During a large scale drill, including external operators, it was noted, by the surveying authority, that the crew performed very well in all aspects. The crew could therefore be assessed as duly competent. There are no reasons to doubt this according to what is known from official documentation. Thus this is merely another falsehood presented to support the official narrative and is easily unveiled.

# The casualty and survivors' testimonies

What can be extracted from survivors' testimonies gives a delineation of the chain of events culminating in the final sinking of the vessel. Moreover, testimonies that strongly contradict the official version appear and are abundant.

There are two things to consider regarding the process of the sinking of the vessel. Firstly, and most importantly, the behaviour of the vessel when the chain of events were initiated. And secondly, how testimonies from survivors can be put in relation to this.

Almost immediately observations and experiences emerge that demand a renewed analysis of the events that unfolded. Furthermore a proper stability review needs to be conducted in relation to the apparent time lapse of the casualty.

# A flooded car deck and related consequences thereof

In simple terms a flooded car deck causes the effected vessel to tilt over relatively rapidly, decreasing the chance of survival significantly for passengers and crew, especially for those residing further down in the vessel. On the M/V Estonia there were cabin compartments for passengers below the car deck, i.e. deck 1. This is essential in relation to the casualty due to the fact that 21 passengers living in these quarters survived. Out of a total 137 survivors there were thus 21 living below the car deck. Thus it can be concluded that survivors from deck number one are overrepresented among the survivors. As previously mentioned, a flooded car deck would have caused the vessel to tilt over apace, making it virtually impossible for anyone living on deck one to survive. It is a notable discrepancy that so many of the inhabitants on deck one managed to reach the higher decks and escape to safety, when in fact they should all have been doomed. Also to be mentioned is that even a few degrees heel of a vessel makes it extremely difficult for a person to move, let alone manage to escape several decks upwards. So how did these 21 passengers manage to reach the outer decks of the vessel in time and ultimately survive?

## *The big heel*

The chain of events were initiated when a significant and massive heel occurred suddenly and threw passengers and crew members alike out of beds, into walls, furniture and other objects. Whereas the majority of passengers and off-duty crew became aware that something was not right in conjunction with this, the passengers on deck one seem to have been aware of troubles before the big heel. Testimonies from these survivors also indicate that two uniformed crew members had made their way down to deck one, and overheard that they were reporting water on deck one via radio. This was all before the big heel. Thus a vast deviation can be noted in regards to the official version of events.

## Summary of testimonies by survivors from deck one

Several passengers on deck one reported hearing and seeing flushing water in the corridors and also entering their cabins. This was obviously a cause of concern and the mentioned passengers started making their way upward. It can be concluded there was water on deck one, in significant quantities, prior to the big heel.

In addition which furthermore was reported from the aforementioned passengers, was the uprighting of the vessel after the initial violent heel. According to several of them the vessel uprighted itself to a position of almost even keel. It was during this timeframe the possibility to flee to safety emerged.

Further testimonies depict how the vessel then slowly tilted back to starboard and subsequently the course of sinking was then slowly initiated.

As can be easily concluded this is totally incompatible with a flooded car deck that would have caused an almost instantaneous catastrophic tilting of the vessel, with no possibility of any uprighting whatsoever.

## Stability and a damaged hull

The M/V Estonia had three compartments beneath the waterline, i.e. the double bottom, the engine room and storage spaces and the passenger compartments. Flooding of the passenger compartments directly from the outside can not be ruled out, though no such observations exist, except for the observations of streaming water in large amounts.

That which remains more likely is thus damage to the hull further beneath and/ or tanks in conjunction with the passenger compartment.

Catastrophic flooding of a compartment in the double bottom and/or engine compartment would have without a doubt caused an abrupt big heel. But what about the reported uprighting?

As water floods the lower compartments it at the same time causes a lowering of the centre of gravity. This will initially cause an uprighting of the vessel as the down flooding water makes its way through the lower parts of the hull. But, at the same time the buoyancy of the vessel slowly depletes, causing a reoccurring slow tilt back from the gained upright position. The vessel is then lost. A lowered center of gravity can not compensate for the uninterrupted inflow of water beneath the water line, it can only stall it. In this scenario the water flushing the cabin compartments was likely caused by one or more engine compartments beneath being pressurised, thus enabling water to penetrate weak spots in the adjacent deck one.

## *Conclusions*

Thus there exists statements from survivors that with precision describe a sinking initiated by a hole in the hull. Likewise there exists no documented testimonies that would support a flooded car deck as the root cause of the fatality.

The J.A.I.C. never even tried to explain these deviations, on the contrary, they used manipulations and blatant lies to divert all attention away from these uncomfortable facts.

To support this in plane facts there was the survivor **Carl Övberg**. When the Swedish program "Efterlyst" ran a special program regarding the Estonia, this gentlemen called in and vented his rage at the J.A.I.C. The J.A.I.C. had resorted to moving his observations to the car deck, when they in fact were made on deck one.

Mr. Övberg is of Turkish descent and had at the time of interrogation not yet mastered the Swedish language. The J.A.I.C. neglected to provide such an important witness with an interpreter.

On the other hand, The German Group of experts, pursuing their own investigation, provided a translator for Mr. Övberg. As a frequent traveller on the M/V Estonia due to his work as a car salesman, he was very familiar with the interior of the vessel.

In distinct detail he described the chain of events. He awoke due to the sound of flushing water and became alarmed. After lighting a cigarette he noticed that water was streaming into his cabin and subsequently decided to flee. Though the abrupt huge heel stalled him, thanks to the slow uprighting and consequent slow tilting back, Mr. Övberg managed to flee and survive to share his experience.

Furthermore, he even provided his own detailed drawings regarding his escape, all of which are consistent with the alternative sinking scenario.

# The final day in the port of Tallinn

There does not seem to exist any accounts of the final day in Stockholm. However, regarding the final day in Tallinn, there is an abundance of material related to it.

There was a Port State Control conducted by both Swedish and Estonian surveyors during the harbour time of the vessel in Tallinn. What can be noted is that there were two separate reports compiled from the inspections, even though the inspection was conducted as a joint venture between the Swedish and Estonian teams.

A deviation here is the fact that both protocols are signed by the same surveyors, even though the content in the reports differ from each other.

To find a reason for this, which could mean that one of the protocols is a forgery, it is important to find out what has been omitted or altered.

## *The damaged sounding pipe in the alternator engine room*

As it turns out it was a damaged sounding pipe in the above mentioned space that was omitted. What this means practically is that the Alternator Engine department was not sealed against the bottom tanks below. Water intrusion into the bottom tanks below thus would also mean flooding of the Alternator Engine space. This is of course an extremely serious deviation which should have demanded a remedy before the vessel could set sail to Stockholm.

Since there exists no documentation about any action taken to repair the pipe in question, it can be concluded that none was taken what so ever. Furthermore this could explain why everything regarding it was omitted from the final official Port State document. Alas, this deviation may have contributed to the sinking.

## Other findings

Regarding the bow visor and ramp installations no serious observations were noted. The exceptions being damaged seals both on the visor for sealing against the hull, as well as the seals for the ramp against the hull.

But these deviations are not considered so serious that it would demand immediate action. On the contrary, these heavy constructions are commonly plagued by the mentioned problem. At worst it can cause smaller amounts of water to penetrate the car deck. But since all car decks are fitted with what is known as scupper valves, this is seldom an issue. The mentioned valves are non-return valves and have the capacity to handle quite a significant amount of water on the car deck, before any stability issues would arise. Therefor it can be concluded that it is highly unlikely that the seals on the ramp/bow visor installation had anything to do with the casualty.

Motorman **Hannes Kadak** actually observed on a camera in the Engine Control Room water penetrating the ramp along the sides, which is consistent with damaged seals. Especially if there are waves present on the outside, which was the case according to confirmed weather reports. But according to Kadaks drawing, the ramp was in a closed position at the time of the observation.

Since the casualty occurred shortly thereafter, i.e. the big heel, the ramp and bow visor obviously were intact at the time. Engineer Margus Treu sent the panicking Kadak upwards during these moments. No doubt this occurred during the big heel and the following uprighting. This also coincides with Treus own statements, i.e. the bilge pumps had been started.

Thus, in conclusion, there were no significant water volumes on the car deck prior to the sinking. But everything points to the fact that a catastrophic flooding had occurred beneath the water line, the double bottom and/or deck 0.

# Amendments to the final day in Tallinn

Two events also occurred during the final day in the port of Tallinn that require additional mentioning. It is to be noted, none of these were documented in the protocols of the Port State Control. On the other hand, the nature of these events stretch beyond what is due course to be noted in a Port State Control.

## *The bomb threat*

It was never disclosed where the threat originated from. Furthermore there is almost no documentation regarding this. It can be noted that the Estonian police took it seriously enough to at least file a report. But there is no disclosure which actions were taken to call of the threat, which was what subsequently happened.

But this no doubt deserves a mention considering the events that unfolded during the last voyage. In relation, perhaps, another deviation was observed by the aforementioned survivor Carl Övberg.

## *Observations during the final loading of cargo*

According to statements of Mr. Övberg he was running late to the port driving a car. His frequent visits to Tallinn were due to the fact that his source of income was selling used Swedish cars to Estonian customers. Övberg was also well acquainted with ship repairs from previous experiences.

As Mr. Övberg approached the cargo loading area he instantly observed anomalies. Firstly the loading area for vehicles was sealed off. Secondly it appeared to be for the benefit of escorted vehicles. Mr. Övberg also noted that the escorting team appeared to be of military nature, this in regard to that he observed both distinctly military vehicles and uniformed personnel.

From official authorities it is known that the departure of the M/V Estonia was delayed until 19:15, the planned departure being at 19:00. Thus it can be concluded that Mr. Övberg observed something that was not routine, which is supported by the fact of the known delay.

## Conclusions

Of course the above mentioned circumstances are not evidence of any foul play, though naturally, they deserve to be mentioned. In any serious and deeply penetrating investigation all events and circumstances should be thoroughly accounted for. Here, once again, the J.A.I.C. utterly failed leaving more questions than answers which unfortunately is its legacy up to this day.

From aside, it can only be concluded, there were events that took place during the final day that raise several questions. A bomb threat in combination with an undisclosed cargo loading raises concerns that these events could be intertwined.

# Hull integrity and definitions by classification societies

In terms of withstanding external and/or internal flooding of a fluid there are three different standards stipulated by the Classification Societies that apply to all seagoing vessels, regardless of intended route. Thus there are no exceptions made if the vessel is certified for worldwide trafficking, but is set to traffic sheltered waters. Hence, contrary to rumour, the M/V Estonia hereby was no exception.

## Definition of water tight and Water Tight Doors

In short terms these can be described as extensions of the hull available for passage of personnel and loading of cargo. Regarding the M/V Estonia these consisted of hydraulically operated doors on deck 0 and deck 1, as well as the forward ramp.

All mechanisms mentioned are designed to withstand being fully submerged by water, as well as maintaining the highest class of perseverance against fire. In an emergency situation they could all be closed remotely, except the forward ramp that required manual operating of the hydraulic system.

No evidence has ever been put forward to question whether these installations were defect on the M/V Estonia. On the contrary, during the Port State Control, no mention hinting of this was noted in any of the erected protocols. Even if there are two versions, in none of them were there any notes regarding this matter.

Therefore it can be concluded that the Water Tight Doors on the M/V Estonia were fully and adequately operational. However, it should be taken into account that the surveyors observed damaged seals on the hull positioning the forward ramp in upright position. This has no serious implications, but it shows that the surveyors performed a thorough check of the state of the vessel.

## *Semi-Water Tight doors and definition*

It is to be observed that these are the doors that sealed off the car deck from the casing, including elevators and stairways leading both upwards and downwards into the vessel.

Unlike the Water Tight Doors these were electro-pneumatically operated locally with basic push buttons. But, however, during voyages, they were locked remotely to prevent unlawful entry on to the car deck.

As the aforementioned water tight doors these doors were also of class A regarding resistance to fire. Moreover, and this is more important, they were also classified to withstand 10 bars of water under pressure. A usual way to test this is simply to use the vessels fire extinguishing system and spray the doors with 10 bars of pressure.

No remarks were made about these doors during the Port State Control, neither regarding functionality or integrity.

## Weather proof classification

This is the third classification regarding hull integrity and basically only stipulates that the adjacent seal needs to withstand regularly occurring harsh weather, i.e. stormy weather with heavy rainfall for example.

This is the case regarding the bow visor on the M/V Estonia. The reason for this is that the inner ramp must be watertight according to classification, thus preventing any leakage from the visor entering the car deck.

Here again there is no deviation in conjunction with the M/V Estonia. Though, as noted earlier, the seals for the ramp were damaged. Indeed, this enabled water from the visor bilge to enter the car deck. But, as will be shown, this was insignificant related to the casualty.

## The car deck and adjacent spaces

Every car deck is equipped with what is known as scupper valves. These are non-return valves designed to lead excess water on the car deck out to sea. During usual operations it is, for example when cleaning the car deck with water, a simple and efficient way to remove unwanted water from the car deck.

As we know from motorman **Hannes Kadak**, he saw some water penetrating the forward ramp. But what can be concluded is that those amounts would in no way overcome the capacity of the scupper valves, thus this never posed a threat to the vessel in terms of stability.

Even if the scuppers had failed, the semi-water tight doors would have withstood the incoming water, preventing any down flooding taking place. But, since it is known from testimonies from surviving

85

passengers and crew, no such flooding could have taken place prior to the big heel.

## The big heel and the engine room crew

Here perhaps the strongest evidence lays that a flooded car deck was not the root cause of the fatality, in combination with testimonies from survivors living on deck one

Hannes Kadak is already in full panic due to the big heel that occurred suddenly, shutting down the engines due to low oil pressure.

**Marcus Treu** thereafter sends Kadak and **Henrik Sillaste** to the emergency escape routes via the funnel. Treu himself remained in the Engine Control Room and performed bilge pumping. These statements were subsequently removed from later interrogations. The reason for Treu omitting those events in subsequent interrogations is unknown, but for sure his initial statements contradict the official description of the chain of events.

## Consequences of the statements

Since it is not possible to pump water from the car deck, or deck 1 for that matter, Treu must have initiated pumping from deck 0. This appears to be shortly before Sillaste and Kadak fled through the funnel emergency escape route.

And most notable, Kadak and Sillaste fled while the forward ramp was closed, according to their own testimonies.

This is direct evidence that the flooded car deck is a complete falsehood. And, as shown, in conjunction with testimonies from deck 1 survivors, everything points to a catastrophic hole in the hull beneath the water line.

# The rescue operation and subsequent findings

Anomalies during the aftermath of the disaster are to be found in the rescue efforts. Though, it must be noted, that the weather changed to more severe conditions that were present during the sinking itself. Most notably the on duty Turku rescue station seems to have been unavailable for radio traffic during the critical initial response to the casualty. The reason for this has never been established and therefore remains a mystery.

An initial testimony is that of the Captain of the M/V Mariella which came to assist with the rescue operation. In the radio traffic it is clearly heard that the Captain, Mr. **Thörnroos**, states that he has a visual sighting off the M/V Estonia. Since this is after the Mayday request made by **Andres Tammes** on the M/V Estonia, it appears that at least the M/V Mariella was relatively close to the scene of disaster.

What is even more peculiar is that Mr. Thörnroos can be heard asking the position of the M/V Estonia even though he already has a visual sighting of the vessel in question. It should be mentioned that Mr. Thörnroos later withdrew the statement in question and proclaimed it to be a "misunderstanding". But it is quite clear from the preserved audio that it can not be contributed to "a misunderstanding", this since he repeats the question several times.

Further on it will be cause to return to the M/V Mariella and the handling of rescued survivors.

## *The vanished rescue boat*

Several survivors who had reached the outer deck reported that a small vessel, obviously belonging to the M/V Estonia, was already making its way from the scene of the disaster.

Since the descriptions of it is that the vessel was enclosed it can be concluded that it was a **MOR**-vessel, Means Of Rescue, designed to haul life rafts and such after being launched.

Launching of such a vessel is relatively time consuming so it must therefore have been launched early on in the chain of events that were about to unfold, or astonishingly, if it is true, prior to the damage that occurred to the M/V Estonia.

According to eye witness accounts the rescue boat headed away from the scene making no effort to assist survivors already in the water or those clinging to operational or failed rescue equipment.

The fate of the rescue boat and the person/persons occupying it remains to be accounted for. Other rescue equipment, most notably life boats, were subsequently found, even many years after the disaster.

A question to be put forward is what if there were individuals on board who knew beforehand what was going to unfold, thus providing their own escape by means of the enclosed MOR-vessel. Obtaining evidence that this was the case is a difficult task of course, but several survivors noticed the aforementioned vessel setting off by itself, whereas instead it could have been of significant use during the rescue operation that was soon to be initiated.

## *Testimonies of rescued passengers*

Survivors who were taken on board the M/V Mariella soon became aware of the fact that they were not being treated according to protocols. On the contrary, according to statements, they almost immediately became subjected to questioning by uniformed personnel. Personnel obviously not belonging to the regular crew. Hence, this unaccounted for personnel had to have been flown in just for this purpose. The obvious and frightening question being, from where?

In particular one woman felt like they were being treated as criminals. They were forbidden to interact with the passengers and crew of the M/V Mariella and barely received any medical assistance. In her own words, she got the feeling that nobody was meant to have survived the sinking of the M/V Estonia.

This is noteworthy, what could constitute such a harsh treatment of traumatised survivors, unless the uniformed interrogators were actually looking for specific details?

To emphasise what the woman in question felt, according to her testimony, she broke down in tears once she reached the safe haven of the Central Hospital in Mariehamn, the Åland Islands.

It is still unknown up to this day who these interrogators were.

## *The missing survivors*

When large scale catastrophes occur it is natural that, especially in the initial stages, wrongful information is spread due to human factor such as stress, confusion and the number of people involved in the process.

However, it has to mentioned, that in the case of the aftermath of the M/V Estonia, perhaps not all initial reports can be contributed to the previously mentioned reasons.

**Sirje Piht**, the widow of **Captain Avo Piht**, claimed right up until the end of her life that she had received a phone call confirming that her husband had survived and was under treatment in Turku, Finland. Following this she also vividly recalled a phone call from her husband, where he is to have stated that all is okay and that he was in a safe place. Though he could not return because of the issues, and that Mrs. Piht has to think of "something overwhelming".

A more disturbing case is that of the Security Guard who initially was listed as a survivor. His brother, then living in Turku, claims that he was called and even met his brother in the Turku Central Hospital. But during the subsequent visit, the information was that the brother in question had been relocated to another ward located in another institution. Finally, when visiting the new ward in question, the staff informed him that they had never even heard of his brother. Also, the supposed room allocated to him, was cleaned and prepared for another patient and showed no signs of anybody recently occupying the space.

There are several more examples of persons initially reported as survivors just to be be proclaimed as deceased further on. The mentioned examples can be considered to be the most striking among the alleged "missing survivors".

As far as is known, no further investigations regarding the "missing survivors" were ever conducted, except in the case of Avo Piht. The Estonian Criminal Police sent a wanted note to Interpol regarding Mr. Piht in the year 2001.

## *Irregularities regarding the EPIRB buoys*

The M/V Estonia was equipped with two of these devices whose function can be compared to that of what is known as "Black Boxes" in the aviation industry. The abbreviation itself stands for "Emergency Position Indicating Radio Beacons". One week prior to the casualty a check of these buoys was conducted that showed that they were fully operational.

Design regulation stipulates that the equipment mentioned must function, as well as automatically float up to the surface, even after the vessel that these were installed on is submerged in water. Both of M/V Estonias EPIRB:s were subsequently recovered, showing that they fulfilled classification rules.

Another short description of these is that they act as a Voyage Data Recorder, or so was the case in 1994.

To activate, deactivate or service these requires not only training, it also demands access to confined spaces as well as knowledge of the physical location in itself. Such can only be obtained by an outsider directly from the personnel on board responsible for the equipment, making it virtually impossible for outsiders to manipulate the equipment.

As will be shown it can clearly be observed that the EPIRB:s indeed had been subjected to interference after the check-up of them was performed one week prior to the disaster. After the check-up someone had to have **deactivated both of them**, moreover on the evening/night of the casualty. This is shown by the fact that, until this day, the exact route, heading, plot and point of the casualty have never been properly established. Since the devices also recorded radio traffic the conclusion must be that a significant portion of the actual radio traffic preceding the catastrophe can be considered lost forever. As it stands now, only the conversations on channel 16 after the Mayday call was sent are available for analysis. This of course constitutes an unheard of deviation.

Yet again, the question arises whom was responsible for this presumed deactivation. There are no other available options than somebody from the crew, or in further extent, an individual guided or shown the procedure involved by a member of the crew.

So what it boils down to is that there can be made no conclusions regarding the final voyage and included data in relation to this. On the contrary, all that exists is external positioning by other vessels, as well as that of the radio traffic following the Mayday signal.

All that exists is approximations, which excludes a large portion of the doomed voyage. From an analytic point of view this is certainly disastrous and a big obstacle to bringing clarity to the chain of events that unfolded.

# The customs clearance in Stockholm

According to a retired Customs Officer handling arrivals at Värta Hamnen, where the M/V Estonia birthed during her stays in Stockholm, there were instructions from above not to check certain vehicles disembarking from the M/V Estonia.

This alarmed the Officer in question so he decided to perform own checks without authorisation. The gentlemen in question found it peculiar that the drivers appeared to be taken aback by the unconventional checks. He described it as if they reacted and behaved as if he was breaking an agreement. According to his statements, the material he observed was some sort of electro- communication devices.

All through the years the gentlemen in question has requested to remain anonymous. His reason to come forth was conscience, he felt that this deviation from practice was morally wrongful. Plus, that in the worst case, it could even be connected to the disaster itself.

# Testimony by Robert Barestrand

In the year 2023 Robert Barestrand began coming forth with information he claimed to possess regarding the murder of the Swedish Prime Minister Olof Palme in the year 1986. More precisely, the information was aligned to a specific group who planned, arranged and committed the murder.

After some time Robert also presented claims that the aforementioned group was to be held responsible for the sinking of the M/V Estonia. And, in addition, that both events were intertwined.

Robert, however, does not claim to know the exact details regarding the sinking of the M/V Estonia, but can recall events he experienced first hand with the group that can be linked to the disaster.

In the testimony there are several details that do in fact coincide with many of the unexplained events before, during and after the sinking. In the following chapters the testimony will be presented as is, as well as the details that can be considered relevant to the disaster itself.

## *The commencement*

Much of the material is based on direct hand observations and partly attending formal and informal gatherings, as well as randomly overhearing conversations by others possibly involved.

## Testimony as recollected

Robert is clear in stating that his memory is somewhat blurred regarding this matter. One matter he is certain about though, when he came to insight of the plans in development, is that he contacted the Swedish police on the 26th of September, i.e. the day the M/V Estonia set sail to Tallinn for the last time. In his own words he told the police that the vessel would be pickled. By speaking to Robert the time of his call can be pinned down to the evening of the 26th of September, after the M/V Estonia had left port.

Another matter Robert is quite certain about is the motive, or at least in part. On board the M/V Estonia were 63 civil servants of the police authority in Stockholm of whom only 5 eventually survived. These had to be, in brute terms, eliminated. They are supposedly to have been shot during the voyage, probably as the chain of events leading up to the disaster were beginning to unfold.

What caught Roberts suspicion prior to the casualty was that he was both shown and observed unusual equipment during his stays with certain members of the group. Among other items there were for example emballages, electronic and digital equipment.

Moreover Robert recalls that a small motor vessel was acquired in connection with the previous mentioned equipment. There was also, here Robert is uncertain, a specific vehicle the group wished to send on board the M/V Estonia. It is unclear if such became the case.

On board the vessel itself on the final voyage, Robert claims, there were people who were aware of what was going to unfold, including both passengers and members of the crew.

# Parts of the testimony that can be corroborated

It is a fact that some sort of bomb threat was obtained on the 27th of September while the M/V Estonia was birthed in Tallinn. Details regarding this are scarce, though one possibility is that the Swedish police forwarded Roberts warning to their Estonian counterparts. It is almost certain that Roberts call was placed after the M/V Estonia had departed from Stockholm on the 26th of September, probably during the later evening. It is a possibility Roberts call is the root origin of the forwarded bomb threat placed on the 27th of September in Tallinn.

There are no reports of gun shots being heard during the fatality, though this does not exclude anything given the circumstances. However, there does exist a report from a diver who participated in the subsequent excursions to the wreckage. On the bridge bodies were found, among them the unknown man in the purple costume. This individual had been seen by passengers interacting with the two captains on board, more precisely dining in one of the restaurants. The diver claimed the man had clear signs of gun shot wounds. It can therefore not be ruled out that several others on board became victims of gun violence.

If in fact the reason for the fatality was blatant sabotage, the natural approach would be to cause damage to the hull below the water line. The quite significant amount of equipment, as well as the specifics of these, Robert observed could very well be linked to such a course of action. It is to be added that Robert also had observed equipment for diving.

An explanation for the deviation regarding the EPIRB buoys can perhaps also be extracted from Roberts testimony. If there were both passengers and crew with advance knowledge of what was about to unfold, it could explain the mysterious deactivation of the EPIRBS:s as well as the unaccounted for MOR-vessel seen leaving the scene of the catastrophe. And as mentioned earlier, it must have been launched in good time prior to the initiating of the sinking.

94

## Summary

It is extremely difficult to obtain concrete evidence in the case of M/V Estonia due to many factors. For one the authorities maintain their stances of keeping silence. For another unheard of actions have been taken on account of several governments, for example the prohibition of diving at the wreckage. It has also come alight that several unofficial, presumably military such, diving excursions have taken place. Military vessels not connected to the official investigation have been sent to the coordinates of the wreckage. And that list goes on, clearly something out of the ordinary has been going on. But mainly thanks to survivors' accounts that are publicly available, and in addition whistleblowers like Robert in this case, at least a plausible alternative scenario is possible to deduct and thereafter present compelling arguments and evidence in favour of it.

## Ending notes

Testimonies from surviving passengers and crew can be obtained at the site

www.estoniaferrydisaster.net

Robert Barestand manages a home page titled www.ynglingen.se and also a direct linked English equivalent www.english.ynglingen.se

# Epilogue

It is said that truth is stranger than fiction. Applied to this writing some may find it overwhelming to grasp that one single individual has experienced such stunning events. In particular the murder of Olof Palme, but also the Estonia ferry disaster, have given rise to a wide range of speculations throughout the years. Even till this day there are seminars, books written, podcasts, Youtube channels as well as other platforms discussing these issues in a broad array of perspectives.

That which differs regarding Roberts denunciations related to the above, is that the experiences are first hand and witnessed. This applies particularly to the case of the Palme murder, although most certainly also to the Estonia matter, albeit not as graphically. It can be described as unique in the history of the aftermath related to both the events.

Not that claims and statements of inside knowledge have been lacking in connection with these immense events, but none of these have ever survived a profound screening. Thus it can not be emphasised enough how Roberts statements differ from the aforementioned.

Having actually been present at the scene of the crime, the murder of Olof Palme, making observations as well as knowing those involved, is simply unprecedented. As the same individuals are said to be responsible for the sinking of the M/V Estonia, it is therefore nothing short of a bombshell being delivered.

Since, especially concerning the Palme case, Roberts declarations can in several instances be corroborated, it must therefore be concluded that the statements are self-experienced. Returning to M/V Estonia Roberts information there can be verified in a more implicit sense, though this in no way degrades the value of the statements in question.

Being intertwined with those responsible also presented Robert with the true underlying motives. Following the Murder of Olof Palme rapid changes to the nation took place. From being a sovereign country where big finance was kept under control for the benefit of the people, the country was transformed into a cesspool by extreme neoliberalism.

From Olof Palmes speech at the Social Democratic party congress in 1984:

*"From the beginning we may have been somewhat nonplussed before this onslaught from the right with all the misleading slogans about freedom. Now neoliberalism is starting to lose its grasp. These ideas have now been tested in practice. All that has come out of it is widened gaps, increased unemployment, social dismantling and worsened state finances.*

*They have tried to make the people believe that all these unpleasant things are necessary elements in an economic policy of crisis. We have up till now been able to show that an economic crisis can be overcome without social dismantling. If we succeed, it is of great importance not only for the citizens of Sweden, but also for the international debate as a whole regarding these issues. Therefore our responsibility is great.*

*It appears the political agitation on the bourgeois at the moment has, as well as in 1982, been overtaken by combat groups, advertising agencies, organisations and more, all in one way or another represented by so called big business..."*

Wise words indeed from a lost era and the question unfolds, will anybody dare to investigate this aspect? Only time will tell.